For Every Season

West Country ingredients, seasonal recipes, practical advice and information from the farm and garden to the kitchen table.

Edited by Claire Allen

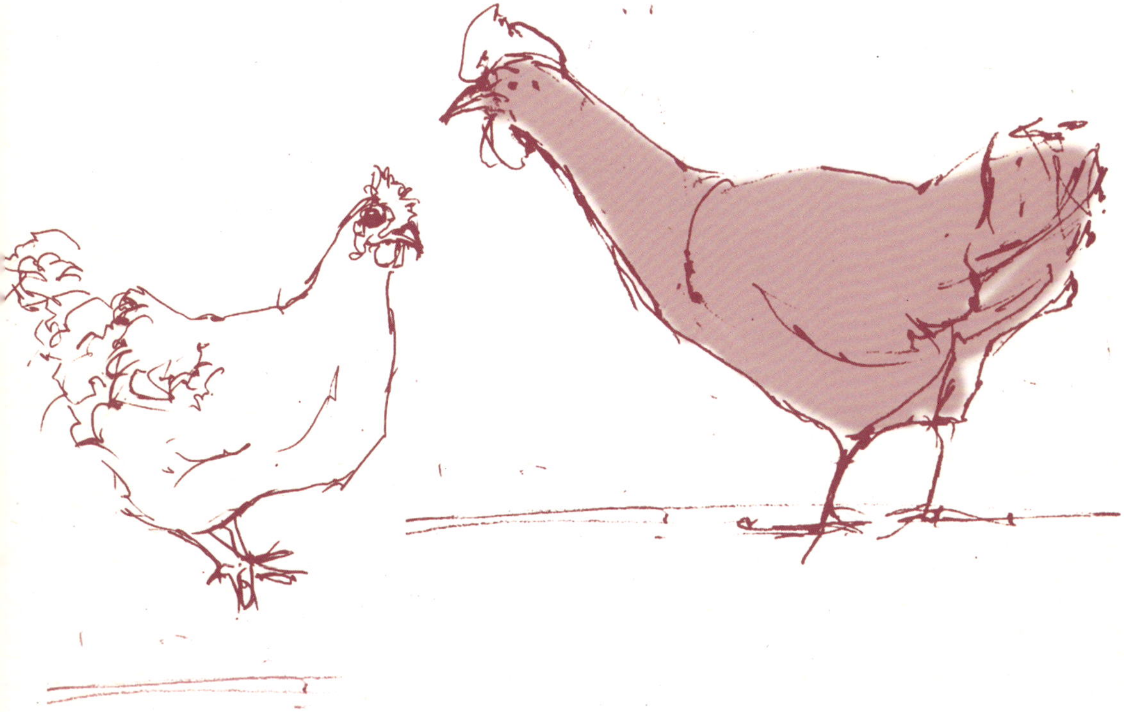

the cookery school at Bordeaux Quay

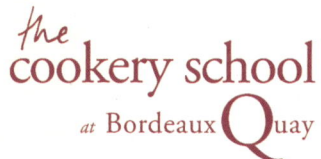

Thank you...

...to Dean Purnell at the Real Design Company who received our first ideas with gentle enthusiasm and since then has worked tirelessly and sensitively on the book's layout and design.

...to Caroline Back who waited so patiently for instructions before producing illustrations more beautiful and fitting than we could have hoped for.

...to Mark Taylor who set the wheels in motion and who spent much of his (hard to come by) spare time proof-reading the end result.

...to the Cookery School and its staff who contributed much more than just inspiration. Time, ideas, recipes and expertise.

...to Claire Allen, the manager of the Cookery School at Bordeaux Quay, who edited this book. This job involved a great deal of work. I am deeply indebted to Claire. There are understatements and understatements. These two last statements belong in the latter category.

And finally, to each and every chef, cook and food writer who contributed their recipes. They receive requests like ours every day and it must be easy to cast the letters aside and forget them. That they replied with genuine interest and sent such wonderful words and recipes, has allowed us to achieve what we set out to do.

Without these people, there would be no book. Thank you.

Barny Haughton

Foreword by Prue Leith

This book is a sum of lots of different parts. There are recipes - some of which take time, others you can make from start to finish in half an hour. There's a list of favourite cookery books, tips on gardening and ideas on what to keep in your storecupboard.

At the heart of it, however, is Food Education – the single most important objective of the Cookery School and a little phrase bandied around frequently by politicians, teachers and celebrity chefs. It sounds worthy and boring and a bit too much like hard work. But what does it mean?

It could be as little as growing a pot of parsley on your windowsill. Or making soda bread with a class of nursery school children. Or as big as teaching a group of young people in care how to shop and cook once they've moved into their own home. Or spending the day with Young Carers – children who have sole responsibility for the care of a parent or relative - picking fruit, vegetables, herbs and flowers at a local walled garden. Or working with school cooks to inspire them to produce better, healthier food for children.

Start small. Instead of buying meat at the supermarket, visit your butcher and ask him where it comes from. Plant a window box of herbs – lavender, rosemary and parsley thrive outside with a bit of watering. Cook an omelette with your children, or make a pot of jam (you don't need to pick kilos of fruit – a punnet of over-ripe strawberries and some sugar is all you need). Roast an organic chicken and make stock from the carcass. Use that stock to make soup or risotto – and you've got another meal. Think before you throw away food. Use it up or buy less next time.

As idyllic as this all sounds, it's nothing new or special or difficult to achieve. It might take a bit of thought and effort at the start but with time and practice it becomes second nature.

Does all this sound rather too worthy? Well, maybe. It needs to be if we are to avoid a gloomy future. But worthy does not mean dull or boring. Anything but!

Because there is, I honestly believe, more fun, satisfaction and pure pleasure to be had in cooking, in teaching, in growing, in sharing food, in sitting down with friends and family over a meal, than this modern, overstressed, junk-ridden world dreams of.

Prue Leith

For Every Season | 5

Contents

Introduction	7
Shopping and Cooking	8-9
Your storecupboard	10
Your kitchen	11
Conversion charts	12
Your garden	13-14
Spring	15-32
Summer	33-50
Autumn	51-68
Winter	69-83
Booklist	84-85
Organisations and initiatives	85
Recipe index	86-87

Introduction

I am writing this in early July 2008. By the time you read it, the global and local food story will have moved on just a little bit more. We will know more about the challenges facing this world of food and little more about some of the solutions. Our own shopping, cooking and eating habits will have shifted a little too. Whether we are a Government or an average family, we will be responding to this newly emerging food reality. Whether we like it or not.

If this sounds pretty dismal, the rest of this book doesn't and there is a very simple premise to this: learning how to cook with ingredients which have been grown with care and which come from near where you live, perhaps even your own garden, is to realise both the pleasure and common sense of what you are doing.

It really is as simple as that. I have just made a salad of potatoes and broad beans from an organic grower in Wells market. In the time it takes to write this paragraph, I washed, thinly sliced (1 minute) and lightly blanched four potatoes in half an inch of simmering water, (1 ½ minutes) podded (1 ½ minutes) and blanched (30 seconds) 500g beans (net weight 100g) in the same water, tossed the vegetables together, still warm, with mint from the garden, olive oil and a squeeze of lemon juice, sprinkled the whole lot with a tiny bit of Maldon sea salt (30 seconds). And I ate this salad with a Cherry Tree Farm soft cow's milk cheese and some home-made whole meal bread. A delicious meditation on the joy of simple, real food.

Cooking like this is a massive antidote to the stresses and anxieties of everyday life. It is a gentle wander in the meadow rather than the stop start misery of traffic in rush hour and when isn't it rush hour now? It is food for our souls as well as our bellies. And it is about more than just food because when you cook like this you see other things differently too.

The fact that it may also be a small part of the solution to the problems of climate change, energy, transport and other minor global issues is almost irrelevant: If all it does is give greater pleasure and meaning to the tricky business of life, then surely this is enough.

Barny Haughton July 2008

Shopping and cooking
A few tips

We need to make more time for both these activities and, like so many things, it's mostly about getting into the habit. At Bordeaux Quay we have a number of ways of working towards a more sustainable kitchen. We work closely with our suppliers to get the freshest, most local, seasonal ingredients and encourage them to use reusable and recyclable packaging. We make the most of our ingredients, using vegetable trimmings and bones for stock for soups, stews, sauces and risotto. We source sustainably by choosing delicious but less used meats such as mutton and offal to make sure that the most is made of every animal.

It's a different story at home, of course, but there are many things you can do to change the way you shop and cook. Below are a few ideas to try as well as lists on what to keep in the kitchen and larder. The lists are by no means exhaustive – treat them as a guideline to organising your kitchen. To equip yourself to this level requires commitment and an initial outlay but it's a starting point you won't look back from and with a little practice and confidence, will soon become a way of life.

Shopping

- Know where what you buy comes from: fish, meat, vegetables, coffee: everything comes from somewhere. Adopt the Slow Food principle of Good, Clean and Fair (tastes good, no chemicals and pesticides, gives the producer a fair wage).

- Buy what's fresh, local and organic, whether at a supermarket or farmers' market.

- What you buy should determine what you cook and eat, not the other way round.

- Buy food with less or at least recycled or biodegradable packaging. This is difficult. But think: packaging is a huge and largely unnecessary waste of energy and materials and millions of tonnes of it goes to landfill.

- Support local producers, farmers, retailers, markets. They are the future of real food and should be at the heart of the local economy.

Cooking

- Good home cooking requires planning ahead, resourcefulness, flexibility and knowing what you have in your fridge. One third of the food in our fridges gets thrown away.

- Think creatively and before it's too late about what to do with leftovers....

- .....Even better, don't have leftovers, unless you have a plan for them: cook the right amount of rice for the meal in hand.

- If vegetables look tired, cook them. Don't let them rot. You can eat them tomorrow, baked in the oven with grated cheese on top.

- Eat less meat but eat good meat: it's better for your health and better for the environment.

- See water and energy as the precious and limited resources they are. Don't leave taps running, preheat the oven for the minimum time.

For Every Season

Your storecupboard

Oils: extra virgin olive, olive, sunflower, groundnut, sesame

Vinegars: red wine, white wine, balsamic, rice wine

Mustards: Dijon, wholegrain, English

Salt: Maldon sea, table, cooking

Sugar: soft brown, white, caster

Flour: plain, self-raising, strong, pasta - tipo oo, corn

Baking powder, bicarbonate of soda, cream of tartar

Grains: semolina, couscous, polenta

Dried pasta: spaghetti, linguine, tagliatelle, penne

Pulses (dried or tinned): borlotti, cannellini, flageolet and butter beans, yellow split peas, lentils, chickpeas

Rice: long grain, pilaf, basmati, Arborio or Carnaroli risotto rice

Tinned fish: anchovies in olive oil or salt, sardines, tuna

Capers: salted (small ones are best)

Olives: black or green

Dried mushrooms: porcini

Chocolate, cocoa powder: good-quality 70% cocoa solids

Nuts: ground, blanched, whole almonds, hazelnuts, walnuts, pecans, Brazil

Dried fruits: raisins, sultanas, currants, apricots, cranberries, prunes

Stem ginger in syrup

Alcohol: sherry, marsala, Madeira, brandy, port, red and white wine

Preserves: marmalade, honey

Misc: soy sauce, fish sauce, oyster sauce tinned, whole, peeled plum tomatoes, sun-dried tomatoes (dried or in oil), pesto, black olive tapenade

Herbs and spices

Black pepper	Bay leaves
Dried chillies	Bouquet garni
Nutmeg	Dried oregano
Cloves	Dried sage
Coriander seeds	Fennel seeds
Cumin seeds	Vanilla pods
Caraway seeds	Cayenne pepper
Turmeric	Fenugreek seeds
Cardamom pods	Garam masala

Fresh

Lemons and limes	Chillies
Garlic	Potatoes
Ginger	Fresh herbs
Onions and shallots	Carrots

To keep in the fridge

Eggs
Cheese: cheddar, Parmesan, feta
Milk
Salami and/or chorizo

Your kitchen

Knives
A set of knives: but the best you can afford, to include
Large cook's knife (24cm blade)
Medium knife (15cm blade)
Small knife (10cm blade)
Palette knife

Tools
Swivel-top peeler
Sharpening steel
Meat thermometer (not essential but handy)
Skewer
Stainless steel box grater
Sieves (1 tin or stainless steel, 1 plastic)
Corkscrew
Slotted spoon
Wooden spoons
Plastic spatula
Whisk
Fish slice
Flexible tin spatula (not essential but handy)
Pastry brush
Potato masher
Ladle
Rolling pin
Lemon juicer
Pestle and mortar
Set of measuring spoons
Pasta rolling machine

Boards
2 heavy wooden chopping boards (one large)

Saucepans
Buy the best heavy stainless steel saucepans you can afford. They don't burn or stick and do wonders for your cooking.
Large saucepan and lid
Medium saucepan and lid
Small saucepan and lid
Good-quality casserole with lid
Non-stick frying pan

Tins
22cm tart tin with removable base
Roasting tin
Baking sheet
2 x 20.5cm cake tins

Bowls
4 different-sized mixing bowls
Pie dish
Measuring jug

Electrical
Food processor (such as Magimix)
or mixer (such as Kenwood or Kitchenaid)

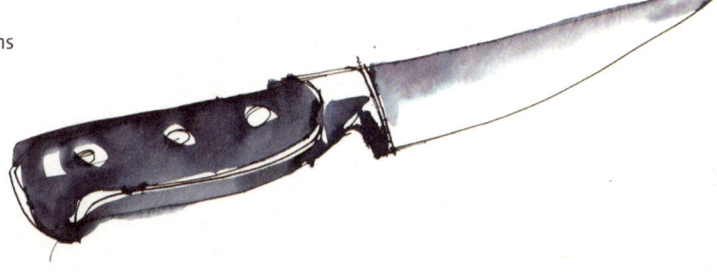

CONVERSION TABLE

Metric	Imperial
7-8g	¼ oz
15g	½ oz
20g	¾ oz
30g	1oz
55g	2oz
85g	3oz
110g	4oz
140g	5oz
170g	6oz
200g	7oz
225g	8oz
255g	9oz
285g	10oz
310g	11oz
340g	12oz (3/4 lb)
370g	13oz
400g	14oz

CONVERSION TABLE

Metric	Imperial
425g	15oz
450g	16oz (1lb)
560g	1 ¼ lb
675g	1 ½ lb
785g	1 ¾ lb
900g	2lb
1kg	2lb 4oz
1.15kg	2lb 8oz
1.35kg	3lb
1.8kg	4lb
2.3kg	5lb
2.7kg	6lb
3.2kg	7lb
3.6kg	8lb
4kg	9lb
4.5kg	10lb

LIQUID MEASURES

1tsp	5ml	
2tbsp	30ml	1 fl oz
¼ pint	150ml	5 fl oz
½ pint	290ml	10 fl oz
¾ pint	425ml	15 fl oz
1 pint	570ml	20 fl oz

LENGTHS

Metric	Imperial
1cm	½ in
2.5cm	1in
5cm	2in
15cm	6in
20cm	8in
30cm	12in

Your garden

Start growing today
We need to eat to nourish our body. The food we eat comes from the soil in one way or another and the soil is just like us, it needs to eat as well. Vegetable and animal waste made into compost gives the soil most of what it needs to be healthy and to grow healthy food. As with all other life on the planet the only other essential ingredient is water. It's really that simple. With a small piece of lawn, a backyard or even a hanging basket, you can begin growing today.

WHERE TO START...

Feed your soil
Keep all your vegetable waste, be it tea bags, egg cartons, cut grass or weeds (as long as there are no seeds clinging to them). Mix them up in a compost bin or even a wooden box will do. Add to this whenever you can, mixing well after every addition. Mixing encourages airflow which helps break it down into compost. If it feels a bit dry then add a little water. Two months before you want to use the compost, stop adding to it but continue to mix it up weekly. This should give you at best, a fresh, coarse compost which will help your fruit and vegetables to grow. If you don't have much compost at the end of this then buy some organic liquid manure and feed the plants as they grow or buy animal manure to give the soil a real boost.

Plant some seeds
The best time to start planning your garden is the end of the year. You'll have time to get the compost going, work out where to plant, prepare the ground, buy seeds and sundries and read lots. A combination of healthy, well-fed soil in a sunny spot (South or West facing) will produce the best result. Without sun, the plants will grow upwards, tall and spindly, in search of sun. They'll still fruit but a brighter, warmer position will produce a more consistent, healthier yield. To get seeds off to a healthy start and speed up the germination process, plant them in seed trays or pots and sit on a sunny windowsill or in a greenhouse. Once the seedlings are strong enough, transfer them gently, roots and all, outside. If you have a yard or balcony, use wooden veg boxes from the greengrocer or even old car tyres instead of buying grow bags. Line whatever container you have with a plastic bag, pricked a few times to encourage drainage, and fill it with soil and compost.

What crops to choose?
The seeds you plant depend on the space you have. Below is an easy guide to which crops work where.

Hanging baskets
Hang baskets outside your house or on a balcony. For a ready-made salad, plant vine cherry tomatoes (in as much sunlight and warmth as there is) around the outer edge of one basket and basil in its centre. In another, plant salad leaves and herbs and in a third, try strawberries.

Window boxes
Herbs, salad leaves and lettuces will thrive on a sunny windowsill as well as cherry tomatoes, radishes, dwarf green beans, carrots and spring

onions. Beetroot are easy and satisfying to grow – you can eat the tops and then the root. For a more adventurous crop, try chillies and red peppers. Strawberries work well too.

Small gardens
Any of the above with the addition of tomatoes, aubergines, peas, rhubarb, spinach, garlic and shallots. Grow outdoor cucumbers up walls and if you're planting new potatoes, choose earlies or second earlies which mature faster than other types and so free up their plot for other vegetables.

Larger gardens
Any of the above with onions, runner beans, sweetcorn, pumpkins and even raspberries.

Who to share your crops with
Gardeners have little choice other than to share crops with wildlife, rabbits, pigeons, slugs, aphids and flea beetles. This can feel harsh at times and the smaller your plot the greater the percentage of food they might eat so you need simple ways to make sure you get the most from the crop. Cover crops with garden fleece (buy it from good garden centres) to steer flea beetle away from salad and cut off the top and bottom of a milk carton and set over a plant to protect it from birds. Beer traps will help get your slugs drunk and drown, ladybirds are great for aphids, but pinching out growth tips on peas and beans helps too. Plant alternate rows of carrots and onions to ward off carrot fly – the smell of the onion is enough to deter them.

Above all, allow everything to grow in moderation and concentrate on feeding the soil which will produce strong healthy plants.

When to harvest
Start picking crops as soon as you like the look of them, lettuce can be small or you can leave it to grow really big. Potatoes are ready anytime after the flowers have died. The best thing to do is use your patch like a fresh larder, pick what you want for the day or meal. There is nothing more wonderful than eating your own grown food with your family and friends.

Phil Haughton owns and runs organic supermarket, The Better Food Company, Proving House, Sevier Street, St Werburghs, Bristol, BS2 9QS www.betterfood.co.uk

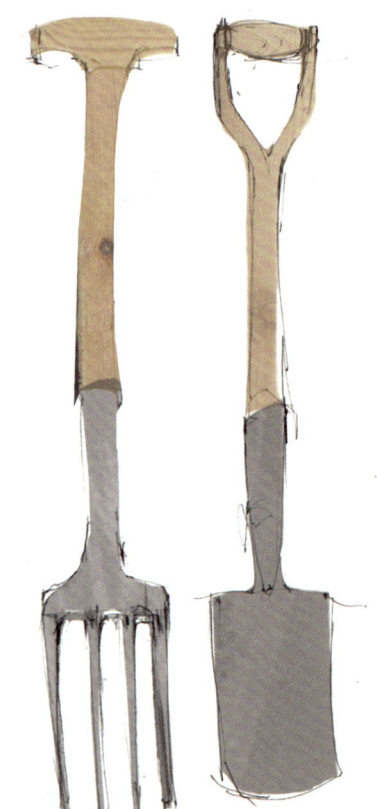

Spring

Beetroot, purple sprouting broccoli along with endless other brassica, nettles, turnips, kohlrabi, leeks and sorrel are the vegetable hallmarks of March. Wild garlic, dandelions, radishes, sea kale and watercress follow in April and by May, radishes, new season beetroot, carrots, fennel and garlic and that short but lovely season of English green asparagus.

But of all the produce these months bring, perhaps the one I love the best is wild garlic. Find it in woods or tucked under hedgerows from late February until April. Pick the leaves young, don't pull the bulbs up. And use the pretty white flowers in salads.

MARCH | APRIL | MAY

Wild garlic mash

"You will find wild garlic growing everywhere at the moment. It's warm and it's March. Here, within cycling distance of Bristol, it can be found in Leigh Woods or Ashton Court, among many other places. It grows in woods, when the leaves on the trees are still just tiny flecks of bright green. Its leaves look a bit like hyacinth leaves. This is because they are related. Pick the garlic leaves as you would spinach, leaving the bulb in the ground for next year. When you get home, wash it well and remove any twigs". Barny Haughton

HANDS-ON TIME: 20 MINUTES
COOKING TIME: AROUND 30 MINUTES
SERVES 8 AS AN ACCOMPANIMENT

1kg potatoes, peeled. The best English potatoes for this - and at this time of year - are likely to be Desiree or Estima; the starchiness which doesn't work for roast or boiled potatoes is perfect for mash.
A big bunch of wild garlic leaves
150ml milk
150ml cream
60g butter

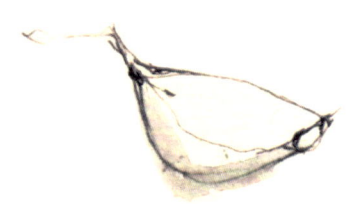

Cook the potatoes in plenty of boiling salted water until tender. Mash well or pass through a fine mouli. Season well.

Coarsely chop the garlic leaves and put them in a pan with the milk, cream and butter. Simmer for a while until the leaves are tender. Leave to cool briefly and then transfer to a food processor or liquidiser until you have a smooth, bright green, creamy liquid.

Beat the liquid well into the mashed potato and maybe add a little more salt and pepper.

You could eat this with a poached egg on top but it goes brilliantly with baked whole lemon-stuffed mackerel or pink roast rump of lamb.

And finally with the leftover mash make a potato and wild garlic soup by letting down the mash to a thick soup consistency with chicken or vegetable stock and a little cream and nutmeg. And then you could poach some eggs and put them gently into each bowl of delicious green soup. If the soup was a pudding, this wouldn't be over-egging it.

cook's tip
Avoid the plants growing along verges of roads or tracks because these are likely to have been visited by passing dogs.

Barny Haughton is chef-proprietor of Bordeaux Quay, V-Shed, Canons Way, Bristol, BS1 5UH www.bordeaux-quay.co.uk

MARCH | APRIL | MAY

Parsley soup with morel mushrooms and crème fraîche

"This soup was the first recipe for my first (and maybe last!) book. It signals the first breath of spring – finding wild morels in the woods is both a surprise and a delight and so often parsley is amongst the first rays of hope in the vegetable garden once spring has started to warm up. Placing the soup over a bowl of iced water is the most important element of the method, as this will retain the brilliant green colour". Sally Clarke

HANDS-ON TIME: AROUND 40 MINUTES
COOKING TIME: AROUND 45 MINUTES
SERVES 4

85g unsalted butter
100ml olive oil
300g potatoes (King Edward or Maris Piper), peeled and cut into walnut-sized pieces
5 celery sticks, roughly chopped
2 medium leeks
2 small heads fennel, trimmed and roughly sliced
400g Italian flat-leafed parsley (approx 3 generous bunches), leaves picked and stalks reserved plus 1tbsp to serve
250g spinach leaves, washed gently and stalks removed
300g morel mushrooms or a selection of wild mushrooms, brushed and broken into even-sized pieces
1tsp thyme leaves, chopped
100ml crème fraîche
6 small sprigs Italian flat-leaf parsley, to serve

Melt the butter in a heavy-based pan with 60ml olive oil. Add the potato, celery, leeks and fennel. Cook gently, stirring until the vegetables have absorbed the oil and butter and are softened but not coloured.

Add the parsley stalks to the pan, season with salt and black pepper and pour over enough water to cover. Bring to the boil, cover and simmer for 20-25 minutes until tender. Add the spinach and all but the tbsp of parsley leaves and bring back to the boil, stirring for 2-3 minutes until the leaves are wilted.

Remove the solids from the pan using a slotted spoon and transfer to a food processor. Whiz to a purée, gradually adding a little of the reserved liquid until a creamy consistency is reached. (You may not need all the liquid – alternatively, you may need to add a little extra water.)

Pass the soup through a medium-fine sieve into a metal container, pushing the solids through with the back of a ladle or spoon.

Put the base of the container into a bowl of ice with enough cold water to come halfway up the side. Stir occasionally as it chills. This immediate chilling will help retain the bright green colour. Taste and adjust the seasoning if necessary.

In a heavy-based frying pan, heat the remaining olive oil and add the mushrooms and thyme, tossing gently, then the remaining tbsp of parsley leaves. Season with salt and black pepper. Set aside. Gently reheat the soup and divide among six warm plates. Serve, topped with a spoonful of mushrooms, a scoop of crème fraîche and a parsley sprig

Sally Clarke's Book, Macmillan. Clarke's, 122-124 Kensington Church Street, London, W8 4BH www.sallyclarke.com

For Every Season | 17

MARCH | APRIL | MAY

Italian bean stew

"For a meatier version, you could adapt this recipe by using pork, ham or chicken stock instead of water to cook the beans and add diced bacon or end bits of ham to add texture and flavour to the body of the stew. A pinch of smoked paprika is good here – but not Italian - so don't call it Italian bean stew". Barny Haughton

HANDS-ON TIME: 30 MINUTES
PLUS 24 HOURS SOAKING
COOKING TIME: 1 HOUR 30 MINUTES
SERVES 6

FOR THE BEANS

500g dried borlotti or cannellini beans, soaked overnight
2 carrots, peeled and chopped into three
2 sticks celery, washed and chopped into three
1 white onion, peeled and halved
1 head garlic, papery skin removed and halved widthways
Bay leaves
Thyme sprigs

FOR THE BASE

1 each red and yellow pepper
2 red onions
1 stick celery
2 medium carrots
2 garlic cloves
1/2 tsp fennel seeds, crushed
Pinch chilli flakes
1/4 tsp saffron
400g can tomatoes
1tbsp tomato paste
1/2 cup white wine
Bay leaves
A few thyme and parsley sprigs

Rinse the soaked beans under cold, running water and transfer to a large pan. Cover with water and add the chopped carrot, celery, onion, garlic, bay and thyme. Bring to the boil then reduce the heat and cook slowly for around 1 hour. Slow-cooking will produce the right, firm but creamy texture. If they cook too fast, the beans will break up and taste chalky. Once the beans are cooked, remove from the heat and leave them to cool in their liquor. Drain, reserving the liquor and discard the vegetables.

To make the base stew, chop the peppers, onions, celery and carrot into bits the size of a 50p piece. Finely slice the garlic. Heat a pan over a gentle heat and add 2tbsp olive oil. Add the chopped vegetables (but not the garlic yet), season with salt and black pepper and cook gently for around 20 minutes until soft and lightly coloured.

Add the sliced garlic and spices and cook for a further 10 minutes until well-amalgamated. Add the tinned tomatoes, tomato paste, wine, bay leaves and thyme sprigs. Season again with salt and black pepper.

Simmer gently until well cooked, adding a little of the bean liquor if it starts to look dry. Add the beans, return to a gentle simmer and leave to cool.

Serve with a drizzle of best-quality olive, a slice of grilled bread and a few parsley leaves.

MARCH | APRIL | MAY

Warm salad of St. George's mushrooms, spinach and tarragon

"The St. George mushroom is a fantastic, native, pale yellow, firm mushroom which is ready to pick on St. George's day – hence the name. They are found in lush pastures rather than woodland so one hopes that the farmers keep the cows out until the short mushroom season is finished. This recipe would work equally well with other varieties of wild mushroom especially Scottish Girolles". Liz Payne

HANDS-ON TIME: 20 MINUTES
COOKING TIME: 20 MINUTES
SERVES 4 AS A STARTER

200g baby spinach leaves
300g St. George's mushrooms
4tbsp olive oil
150g baby shallots, peeled and left whole
2 garlic cloves (new season if possible), peeled and finely chopped
1/2 tsp chopped thyme
1/2 bunch tarragon, chopped
Squeeze of lemon juice

Wash the spinach leaves and pick off any large stalks. Brush the mushrooms and break any large ones in half. Heat the olive oil over a gentle heat and fry the shallots until tender and just golden. Add the garlic, thyme and mushrooms and fry over a high heat for a few minutes. Season and add the tarragon.

Put the spinach leaves in a large serving bowl, add the mushrooms and toss well to mix and soften the leaves. Squeeze over a little lemon juice and serve.

Liz Payne is head chef at Bordeaux Quay, V-Shed, Canons Way, Bristol, BS1 5UH www.bordeaux-quay.co.uk

For Every Season | 19

MARCH | APRIL | MAY

Rhubarb crunch

"This is a good introduction for children to the distinct flavour of rhubarb. The orange and cinnamon help to take the sharpness away. You can use fresh or frozen rhubarb".

Jeanette Orrey

HANDS-ON TIME: 10 MINUTES
COOKING TIME: 50 MINUTES
SERVES 4

FOR THE FILLING
450g forced rhubarb
1 thumb-sized piece pared orange rind
55ml water
1tsp ground cinnamon
2 eggs
55g cornflour
55g golden syrup
475ml milk

FOR THE CRUMBLE TOPPING
55g butter
115g rolled oats
85g brown sugar

Preheat the oven to 190°C (375°F) gas mark 5.

Chop the rhubarb stalks into 5cm pieces and put in a pan with the orange rind. Add just enough water to cover and simmer over a low heat until the rhubarb is tender but still retains its shape.

Remove the orange rind and transfer the fruit and its juices to a deep tin. Sprinkle over the cinnamon.

Beat together the eggs, cornflour and syrup in a heavy-based pan and stir in the milk. Put the pan over a low heat and cook, whisking continuously, until the custard has thickened. Leave to cool slightly then pour over the fruit.

To make the crumble, melt the butter in a pan, stir in the oats and sugar then sprinkle it over the custard. Bake in the preheated oven for about 25 minutes until the crumble mixture is golden.

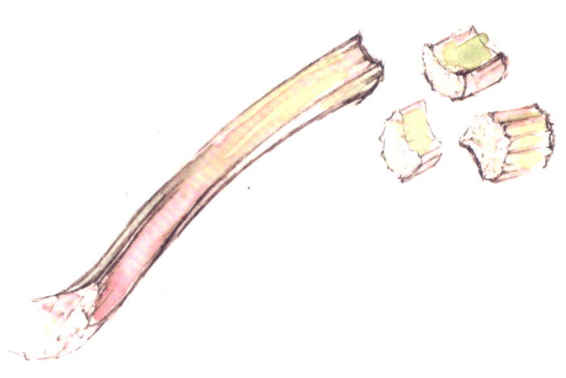

The Dinner Lady by Jeanette Orrey, Bantam Press. Jeanette Orrey inspired and represents The Food for Life Partnership, a countrywide campaign aimed at reconnecting children with their food and its provenance www.foodforlife.org.uk

20 | For Every Season

MARCH | APRIL | MAY

Moroccan chicken tagine

"The subtlety and perfume of a well thought-out tagine are something to cheer up the dullest, coldest night with memories of sunshine and colour". Rick Stein

HANDS-ON TIME: AROUND 20 MINUTES
COOKING TIME: AROUND 25 MINUTES
SERVES 4

2tbsp olive oil
4 x 170g skinless boneless chicken breast
2 celery sticks, chopped
1 carrot, peeled and chopped
1 small onion, peeled and chopped
1/4 preserved lemon, finely chopped
4 Roma or plum tomatoes, finely chopped
570ml fresh chicken stock
8 small new potatoes, cut lengthways into quarters
16 pitted black olives
1tsp coriander, chopped, plus extra to serve
1tsp mint, chopped

FOR THE CHERMOULA

2tbsp coriander, roughly chopped
3 garlic cloves, chopped
1/2 tsp ground cumin
1/2 medium-hot long red chilli, de-seeded and chopped
1/2 tsp saffron strands
85ml extra virgin olive oil
Juice of a lemon
1/2 tsp paprika

To make the chermoula, put all the ingredients in a food processor and whiz until smooth. Season with salt and black pepper.

Heat the oil in a deep frying pan. Season the chicken breasts on both sides with salt and black pepper. Add to the pan and fry over a medium heat for 1-2 minutes until golden then flip over and lightly brown the other side.

Transfer to a plate and set aside.

Add the chopped celery, carrot and onion to the pan and fry over a low heat for 5 minutes until softened but not brown. Add half the chopped preserved lemon, 2tbsp chermoula, the chopped tomatoes and stock. Return the chicken to the pan, then bring to the boil. Reduce the heat to low and simmer for 10 minutes.

Add the sliced potatoes to the pan and cook for a further 6-8 minutes until the potatoes and chicken are cooked through. Stir in the olives, fresh herbs and the remaining chermoula and preserved lemons. Adjust the seasoning if necessary. Lift the chicken into warmed deep plates and spoon over the sauce. Serve with extra torn coriander and steamed couscous.

Rick Stein owns The Seafood Restaurant, St Petroc's Bistro, Rick Stein's Café and Stein's Fish & Chips, Padstow, Cornwall www.rickstein.com

For Every Season

MARCH | APRIL | MAY

Soft pistachio meringue with blood oranges and rhubarb

"At the restaurant we wait all autumn for news of the blood oranges arriving from Sicily. Then when the spring rhubarb arrives from Yorkshire we have the perfect combination! Forget memories of school lunch tinned rhubarb – instead, the young pale pink stalks poached or baked gently in a sweet wine and blood orange syrup make a truly special dessert, arranged prettily on this marshmallow-y meringue". Sally Clarke

HANDS-ON TIME: AROUND 30 MINUTES
COOKING TIME: 40 MINUTES
SERVES 6

3 egg whites
185g sugar
2tsp cornflour
1tsp champagne wine vinegar
1/4 tsp vanilla essence
55g shelled, unsalted pistachio nuts, roughly chopped
200g forced rhubarb (approximately 3 sticks)
55g sugar
85ml blood orange juice
85ml inexpensive sweet white wine, e.g. Jurançon or Beaumes de Venise
250ml double cream, softly whipped
6 large blood oranges, peeled of peel and pith, cut into segments
6 mint sprigs

Preheat the oven to 140°C (275°F) gas mark 1 and line a baking sheet with silicone wax paper.

Put the egg whites in a clean, dry bowl and whisk until stiff peaks form. Gradually add the sugar, whisking continually until thick and glossy. Finally whisk in the cornflour, vinegar and vanilla essence. Fold in the chopped pistachio nuts.

Scoop the meringue into six equal-sized mounds on the baking sheet, leaving a small space between each one as they will puff a little during cooking.

Bake for 40 minutes until crisp but not coloured. The interior should be soft and marshmallow-like.

Meanwhile, prepare the rhubarb. Chop into lengths of 4-5cm and arrange in a single layer in an ovenproof dish. Sprinkle over the sugar and pour over the orange juice and wine. Cover with foil and bake in the same oven for 10-15 minutes until tender. Set aside to cool. Choose and reserve the most beautiful 18 pieces of rhubarb and push the remaining pieces through a plastic sieve with all the cooking juices. Taste and adjust the sweetness if you need to.

To assemble, put a meringue on each plate, top each with a spoonful of whipped cream and arrange the orange segments and reserved rhubarb attractively over the top. Serve immediately with the rhubarb sauce drizzled over and topped with a mint sprig.

Sally Clarke's Book, Macmillan. Clarke's, 122-124 Kensington Church Street, London, W8 4BH www.sallyclarke.com

MARCH | APRIL | MAY

Spinach and anchovy tart

"Perfect at any time of year, but plus perfect in the spring, when you can buy or grow tiny pousse, the baby leaves of spinach that are gently, tenderly unferrous and don't exude copious amounts of liquid when you cook them. Spinach and anchovies: what can I say, other than that they are a heavenly marriage. Don't add salt: the anchovies have it in spadefuls". Tamasin Day-Lewis

**HANDS-ON TIME: 30 MINUTES
PLUS 45 MINUTES CHILLING
COOKING TIME: 45 MINUTES
SERVES 6**

FOR THE PASTRY
110g organic white flour
Pinch sea salt
55g cold, unsalted butter
1tbsp best olive oil

FOR THE FILLING
30g unsalted butter
1tbsp olive oil
350g organic baby spinach
200ml double cream
1 organic egg plus 2 egg yolks
12 anchovy fillets

serving suggestion
Serve with something plain like a cherry tomato salad, and good white country bread and butter.

Sift the flour and salt into the food processor then cut the butter into cubes on top of it. Pulse several times for 3-4 seconds at a time before adding the oil through the feed tube. If the paste is still crumbly, add 1tbsp water. The moment it has cohered into a single ball, stop, remove from the food processor, wrap in clingfilm and chill for at least 30 minutes.

Lightly dust the worksurface with flour. Roll out the pastry with a lightly floured rolling pin to approx 1cm thick. Drape the pastry over the rolling pin and lift over a 23cm tart tin. Ease the pastry into the corners using the side of your finger. Roll the rolling pin across the top of the tin to remove any excess. Chill until firm while you make the filling. Preheat the oven to 190°C (375°F) gas mark 5. Line the pastry case with a sheet of greaseproof paper and fill with baking beans. Bake until the sides of the pastry case are just cooked (around 15 minutes) then remove the beans and paper, prick the base all over with a fork and return to the oven for a further 5 minutes until the base is cooked.

While the pastry is in the oven, heat the butter and olive oil in a heavy-based pan. Add the spinach, season with black pepper and stir briefly for a couple of minutes until the spinach has wilted but not lost its shape.

Whisk the cream, egg and yolks together, then pour in any liquid from the spinach pan. Whizz together the spinach and anchovies in a food processor - you want to keep their texture and not reduce them to a purée. Add to the cream and eggs and stir with a fork. Pour into the pastry case and cook for about 25 minutes. Leave to cool for 10 minutes.

Tamasin's Kitchen Bible, Weidenfeld and Nicholson. A well-loved cook and one of Britain's finest food writers, Tamasin Day-Lewis has produced and directed television documentaries and appeared in several cookery series. Other books include The Art of the Tart and Tarts with Tops on.

For Every Season

MARCH | APRIL | MAY

A proper chocolate cake

"Nothing beats a slice of chocolate cake with a cup of tea, made properly from leaves not bags. It's time for the return of afternoon tea and this simple recipe, adapted from one by Jennifer Paterson (several years before she became one of the Two Fat Ladies), is as good a place to start the campaign as any". Mark Taylor

HANDS-ON TIME: 30 MINUTES
COOKING TIME: 35–40 MINUTES
CUTS INTO 12 SLICES

125g good quality plain chocolate
175g butter, softened
175g soft brown sugar
1tsp vanilla essence
4 large free-range eggs
150g self-raising flour
25g cocoa powder

FOR THE ICING
225g good quality plain chocolate
2 egg yolks

Preheat the oven to 180°C (350°F) Gas mark 4. Grease and line two 20.5cm cake tins. Break the chocolate into a small pan with 3tbsp boiling water. Melt over a very low heat without stirring. Remove from the heat then transfer to a bowl with the butter, sugar and vanilla and cream together with a wooden spoon.

Separate the eggs and add the yolks to the chocolate mixture, one by one, beating well between additions. Sieve the flour and cocoa into the mixture and gently fold in.

Whip the egg whites until stiff peaks form and lightly fold into the mixture. Divide the mixture between the cake tins.

Cook in the centre of the preheated oven for 25-30 minutes. Cool slightly in the tin then turn out on wire racks to cool completely.

To make the icing, melt the chocolate in a small pan with 3tbsp strong coffee (espresso, for example). Add the egg yolks one at a time, beating until thick. Spread half the icing in the middle of the cake and half over the top or leave the top plain for a less rich version.

MARCH | APRIL | MAY

John Dory with kale, cockle and blood orange vinaigrette

"Kale and blood oranges are two of the season's greats, and simply partnered with a beautiful piece of John Dory and a scattering of fat cockles, you have the makings of a simple yet elegant dish. The John Dory could be substituted for something less grand, but to my mind this would be missing the point of the dish's simplicity". Matt Tebbutt

HANDS-ON TIME: 15 MINUTES
COOKING TIME: AROUND 10 MINUTES
SERVES 2–3

Juice of 4 blood oranges
1tsp Dijon mustard
55ml sherry vinegar
150ml extra virgin olive oil
100g cockles, cooked and removed from the shell, cooking liquor reserved
2 medium sized John Dory, filleted
15g unsalted butter
Juice of a lemon
150g kale, picked & washed

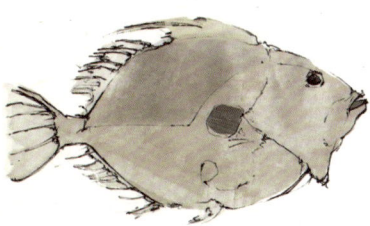

To make the cockle vinaigrette, put the blood orange juice in a small pan and heat gently until reduced to around 1tbsp. Set aside to cool

Put the mustard in a small mixing bowl with the vinegar and 1tbsp water. Pour in the olive oil and stir vigorously to mix. Don't whisk - you don't want to thicken and aerate this too much. Season to taste with salt and black pepper. Add the reduced orange juice, taste again and then stir in the cockles. Set aside in the fridge until needed.

Heat a non-stick pan over a medium heat, add enough olive oil to just cover the base and season the fish with salt and black pepper. Add the fish to the hot pan, skin-side down and cook, over a medium heat, until two-thirds cooked. The flesh will turn from translucent to milky and opaque as it cooks. Flip over and cook the other side. The whole process should take no more than 3-4 minutes. Transfer the fish to a warm plate, top with a knob of butter and squeeze over a little lemon juice. Leave to rest while you cook the kale.

Bring a large pan of salted water to the boil and add the kale. Cook for no more than 1-2 minutes just to remove the bite, then drain. Arrange on a large serving plate. Lay the fish on top of the kale and dress with the cockle vinaigrette. Serve with boiled potatoes.

Matt Tebbutt is chef-proprietor of the Foxhunter, Nantyderry, Monmouthshire, NP7 9DN www.thefoxhunter.com He has presented and appeared in several television series

For Every Season

MARCH | APRIL | MAY

Carrot cake

"I was asked to make a birthday cake for a smart lady in Kensington. She told me in no uncertain terms that she enjoyed carrot cake but "it must be very moist, not like the last one you made". With slightly dented pride, I went to my good friend Elspeth Henderson's house where after a few calming gin and tonics she told me not to worry and produced this amazingly rich, moist and utterly delicious carrot cake recipe. (I'm pleased to say that it met with approval!)". Carol Haines

HANDS ON TIME: 10 MINS
COOKING TIME: AROUND 1 HOUR
CUTS INTO 12 SLICES

FOR THE CAKE
**225g self raising flour
2 level tsp baking powder
150g light soft brown sugar
50g chopped walnuts
100g carrots, washed, trimmed and grated
2 ripe bananas, mashed
2 eggs
150ml corn oil**

FOR THE TOPPING:
**Finely grated zest and juice of 1 lemon
100g softened unsalted butter
100g icing sugar**

Preheat the oven to 180°C (350°F), gas mark 4. Grease and line a 20.5cm springform cake tin.
Sift together the flour and baking powder into a large bowl and stir in the sugar. Add the nuts, carrot and bananas and mix lightly. Make a well in the centre, add the eggs and oil and beat until well blended.
Turn into the tin and bake in the oven for around 1 hour until the cake is golden brown and starting to shrink away from the edges. A skewer pierced into the centre of the cake should come out clean. Turn out, remove the paper, and leave to cool on a wire rack. To make the topping, put the lemon zest and juice in a small pan and bring to the boil. Bubble gently until reduced by three-quarters. Leave to cool. Beat the butter until pale and creamy. Add the sifted icing sugar and the reduced lemon mixture. Beat well and spread over the top of the cooled cake. Leave to harden then cut into slices and serve.

Trained chef, Carol Haines teaches classes for both adults and children at the Cookery School at Bordeaux Quay. She runs her own catering company too.

For Every Season

MARCH | APRIL | MAY

Spring lamb with anchovy mayonnaise and hors d'oeuvres

"This is my most favourite way to eat, lots of little accompaniments to the main event. It's really nothing more than a carnivorous version of 'le grand aioli'. If you're feeling conservative, omit the snails, but I think they bring a certain earthiness to the table. As for the dip, lamb and anchovy are a classic pairing and should never be substituted".

Matt Tebbutt

HANDS-ON TIME: AROUND 30 MINUTES
COOKING TIME: 45 MINUTES – 1 HOUR
SERVES 6-8

1.75 – 2kg shoulder of lamb, bone in
3 fat garlic cloves, peeled and finely sliced
3-4 rosemary sprigs
Olive oil
Butter
1 lemon
1kg new potatoes
400g French beans, topped and tailed
2 bunches English asparagus

TO SERVE: any or all of the following - baby artichokes, black olives, soft-boiled duck eggs, grilled spring onions, 100g freshly cooked snail meat tossed in garlic, shallot and parsley

FOR THE ANCHOVY MAYONNAISE
3 egg yolks
6 anchovy fillets, roughly mashed
6 garlic cloves, crushed
350ml extra virgin olive oil
Small splash Pernod

First, make the mayonnaise. Put the egg yolks, anchovy fillets and crushed garlic in a bowl and mix together. Start adding the olive oil, drop by drop at first and then in a steady stream. Don't pour too quickly as the mayonnaise will split. Season to taste with salt and black pepper and stir in a splash of Pernod. Chill in the fridge while you prepare the lamb.

Preheat the oven to 180°C (350°F) gas mark 4. With a small, sharp knife, make tiny incisions all over the lamb and stud with slivers of garlic and rosemary sprigs. Season with black pepper, drizzle over 2tbsp olive oil and smear over a little softened butter. Squeeze over the juice of a lemon. Roast in the oven for 45 minutes – 1 hour until just pink. Leave to rest in a warm place for at least 30 minutes before serving.

Cook the potatoes in plenty of boiling, salted water until just tender. Drain well and set aside to keep warm.

Blanch the beans in boiling, salted water until just tender. Drain well and set aside to keep warm. In the same pan, blanch the asparagus, taking care not to overcook it (2-3 minutes is long enough). Drain and set aside to keep warm.

Carve the lamb and arrange on a large serving platter with the new potatoes, asparagus and green beans. Dot bowls of black olives, chopped hard-boiled eggs, baby artichokes, snail meat, spring onions and anchovy mayonnaise around the table and let people help themselves.

Matt Tebbutt is chef-proprietor of the Foxhunter, Nantyderry, Monmouthshire, NP7 9DN www.thefoxhunter.com He has presented and appeared in several television series

MARCH | APRIL | MAY

Asparagus and potato frittata

"Fritatta is a kind of Italian omelette and, as with the French version, it works with almost any filling. The best way of making frittata is to use a small oven-proof handled frying pan, which will make enough for two and then repeat the process to serve four".

Barny Haughton

HANDS-ON TIME: 15 MINUTES
COOKING TIME: AROUND 20 MINUTES
SERVES 4

3 medium sized waxy potatoes, peeled
1/2 bunch English asparagus
8 eggs
Small bunch of chives, chopped
100g unsalted butter
2tbsp grated parmesan

Preheat the oven to 200 (400°F) gas mark 6. Cut the potatoes into 5mm slices and cook in a small amount of lightly salted boiling water. Blanch the asparagus and slice into 2cm lengths. Beat the eggs in a big bowl, season with salt and pepper and add the potato, asparagus and chives. Mix well.

Heat half the butter in the pan, coating the sides as well, until almost browning. Add half the egg mix and lower the heat. Cook gently for a few minutes until almost set, loosening the mix at the sides of the pan with a palette knife or spatula. Sprinkle over half the parmesan and place in the oven for 1 minute. Remove, slide on to a plate. Repeat the process with the remaining egg mix. Serve with a green salad of soft lettuce and mustardy dressing.

Frittata should be served at room temperature.

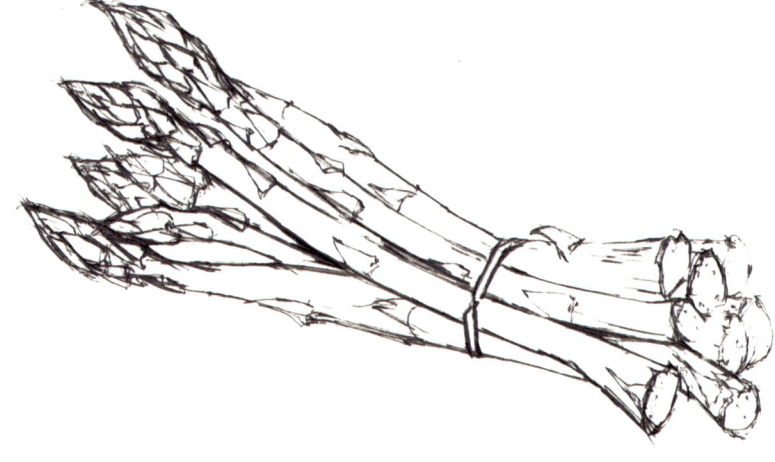

Barny Haughton is chef-proprietor of Bordeaux Quay, V-Shed, Canons Way, Bristol, BS1 5UH www.bordeaux-quay.co.uk

MARCH | APRIL | MAY

The four seasons vegetable potage

"What to do with a veg box full of vegetable strangers? How to celebrate this month's treasure in the garden, allotment or greengrocer? We need a soup base for all seasons. This may not be a refined, classic soup but it'll be delicious and exciting as it defines you as a cook who has a keen sense of season. Always search for what is best and freshest on the day as duff ingredients = duff soup every time". Kate Benson

HANDS-ON TIME: 30 MINUTES
COOKING TIME: 40 MINUTES
SERVES 6

1 large onion, peeled and chopped
1 leek, washed and sliced
1 stick celery, washed and chopped
1 garlic clove, peeled and sliced
1 floury potato, peeled and chopped
50g unsalted butter
1tbsp extra virgin olive oil
1 thyme sprig
1 bay leaf
750g chosen seasonal vegetables, prepped i.e. washed podded or peeled (and diced as above if needed)
500ml chicken or vegetable stock
500ml milk
Juice of 1/2 lemon
Complementary herbs or spices may also be added.

Put the chopped vegetables in separate bowls. Melt the butter and oil in a large heavy-based pan over a low heat. Sweat the vegetables slowly in the following order; onions, leeks, celery and garlic, leaving at least 3 minutes between additions. Cook until soft, then stir in the potato, herbs and the seasonal vegetables. Continue to cook for a further 5 minutes stirring frequently, so that they cook without sticking and burning. The longer you can devote to this part of the recipe the better the flavour of the final soup. Add enough stock and milk to cover the vegetables. Season well with about 1tsp salt and a twist or two of freshly ground black pepper.

Bring to the boil as quickly as possible and simmer with a lid on for about 20 minutes or until the headline vegetable is soft.

For a puréed soup, pour the mixture into a liquidiser and blend until smooth. Taste and adjust the seasoning if necessary. Add lemon juice to taste.

If you want to serve a soup with bits, as my children put it, liquidise a quarter of the soup until smooth and return to the pan. Season as above.

Just before serving, bring to the boil then remove from the heat and pour into serving bowls. Garnish with chervil leaves, chopped parsley, strips of basil, snipped chives or a little lemon zest. You could finish each bowl with a delicate swirl of best quality extra virgin olive oil or a little truffle oil or even a swirl of cream – but not all three!

Kate Benson is one of the valuable and talented teachers at the Cookery School at Bordeaux Quay. Among other courses, she developed and now leads our year-long course – How to Cook with Confidence.

MARCH | APRIL | MAY

Spelt barley risotto with cavolo nero, bacon and Berkswell cheese

"Sharpham Farm estate in Somerset produces organic beef, sheep and cheese (the chalky white and distinctively textured Sharpham Brie, for one). Sharpham also grows spelt barley. Although this brownish/grey coloured ancient strain of wheat doesn't have the starch of risotto rice and so won't produce the creamy texure of a classic Italian risotto, you can treat it in exactly the same way. I am including streaky bacon in this recipe, but it will be just as lovely without". Barny Haughton

HANDS-ON TIME: 20 MINUTES
COOKING TIME: 40 MINUTES
SERVES 4 AS STARTER

1 head cavolo nero or kale
500ml vegetable or chicken stock
olive oil
1 small red onion, finely diced
2 sticks of celery, sliced into very thin 2cm strips
6 chestnut mushrooms, finely sliced
50g streaky bacon, diced
200g spelt barley (or Italian faro will do)
1/4 dried chilli or pinch chilli powder
2 garlic cloves peeled and finely sliced
200ml white wine
25g butter
100g Berkswell or other hard sheep's milk cheese, grated (pecorino is lovely)
Handful flat-leafed parsley, chopped
Juice of 1/2 lemon

Tear the cavolo nero into smallish pieces. Heat the stock until it's simmering gently.

Heat a splash of olive oil in a large pan, add the onion, celery, mushrooms and cook gently until softened and lightly coloured. Add the bacon and cook until just starting to brown, then stir in the spelt. Cook gently for a little longer, stirring all the while, adding the chilli and garlic at the last moment so that it just colours. Now pour in the white wine and cook gently until absorbed. Throw in the torn cavolo nero and stir well. Start adding the hot stock little by little allowing the grain to absorb the liquid as you go, until the grain is firm but yielding at the same time. Remove from the heat. Add the butter, half the grated cheese, half the parsley and the lemon juice.

Serve with more grated cheese and a scattering of parsley.

cook's tip

Remember: whether made with risotto rice or spelt barley, risotto should never be stodgy or lumpen. It should be soft and loose enough to spread beautifully about the plate all on its own.

MARCH | APRIL | MAY

Pollack Grenobloise

"Because it's so readily available, this wonderful fish is seldom treated with reverence. With the chicken stock acting as a perfect background to set off the flavours in the sauce, this recipe illustrates one of many ways an apparently unspectacular fish can be glorified". Raymond Blanc

HANDS-ON TIME: 20 MINUTES
COOKING TIME: 20 MINUTES
SERVES 4

30g country white bread, chopped into cubes, measuring 1cm x 1cm
4 x 175g pollack fillets, skin on, bones removed
4 pinches sea salt
2 pinches white pepper, freshly ground
40g unsalted butter
60ml water
1/2 lemon, peel removed, segmented and juice reserved
2tbsp capers, washed and drained
1 shallot, peeled and finely chopped
15g flat leafed parsley, finely chopped
1 egg, hard boiled, peeled and coarsely grated

To cook the croutons, preheat the oven to its highest setting. Scatter the cubes of white bread on a large baking tray and dry roast in the oven for 3-4 minutes. Remove from the oven and set aside. Reduce the temperature to 200°C (400°F) gas mark 6.

Pat dry the pollack fillets to remove any excess moisture and season with the salt and white pepper. Melt the butter in a large ovenproof frying pan over a medium heat. When it starts to foam, add the fish fillets flesh-side down. Cook for 5-6 minutes until coloured, then carefully flip over the fillets and cook for a further minute. Transfer the pan to the oven for 4-5 minutes.

Remove from the oven and return to a high heat for a minute then carefully lift the fish onto a serving dish.

To make the sauce, add the water to the fish pan to dissolve and emulsify the caramelised juices. Add the lemon segments and juice, the capers, shallot and parsley to the pan and return to the boil. Taste, adjust the seasoning if necessary and pour over the fish. Sprinkle over the grated egg and croûtons and serve.

cook's tip
The flesh and skin of the fish must be dry. If it's wet the fish will boil instead of caramelising.

Raymond Blanc opened hotel and restaurant Le Manoir aux Quat'Saisons in 1984. Since then he has won two Michelin stars, opened a chain of Brasseries and written a selection of best-selling cookery books. Manoir aux Quat'Saisons, Church Road, Great Milton, Oxfordshire, OX44 7PD www.manoir.com

MARCH | APRIL | MAY

And another thing...

Purple sprouting broccoli with chilli olive oil and lemon

You can do this with any of the brassica family (purple sprouting, chard, spring greens, kale etc): for 500g of the vegetable, peel and slice two cloves of garlic, crush a small pinch of dried chilli and fry both for a second in a little olive oil or butter. Add a splash of water, the broccoli or whatever vegetable you've found in the market (leaves torn, stems halved lengthways if very thick), add a pinch of salt, cover and cook gently until just tender. Eat warm with a hard West Country sheep's cheese shaved over it.

Leeks vinaigrette

Simmer small, washed leeks in salted water until soft. Make a vinaigrette with 3 parts olive oil to 1 part lemon juice. Season and toss together while the leeks are still warm. Chop up a couple of semi-soft boiled eggs (about 8 minutes in boiling water) and gently mix with small bunch of snipped chives and serve with the leeks.

Asparagus with hollandaise sauce

(Do not make this sauce if you are in a bad temper)
You will need 200g unsalted butter, 3 egg yolks, 2tbsp white wine vinegar, a pinch of salt and a lemon. You will also need a bowl which will fit over a saucepan of gently simmering water. Put the vinegar in a small pan with a little water and boil gently to reduce it to 2tsp. Leave to cool. Melt the butter and transfer to a jug.

In the bowl, mix the egg yolks and reduced vinegar together with a pinch of salt, set the bowl over the pan of gently simmering water and whisk until the yolks are light and creamy. Remove from the heat and slowly pour in the melted butter, whisking as you go. Add a squidge of lemon juice and check for seasoning. Once made, hollandaise sauce needs to be kept warm to stop it splitting. Put a little pile of blanched asparagus on a plate, top with a poached egg and spoon over the sauce. Or turn the sauce into bearnaise sauce by adding freshly chopped tarragon and perhaps a little Dijon mustard.

Summer

Dandelions, rainbow chard, new season garlic, tomatoes of every kind, beetroot, turnips and carrots, broad beans, peas, green beans, runner beans, girolles, courgettes, courgette flowers, sorrel, strawberries, gooseberries, raspberries, redcurrants, cherries, blackberries, sloe berries, plums, cobnuts, samphire, an endless list. These three summer months bring abundance and variety and with them, joy to every cook and kitchen.

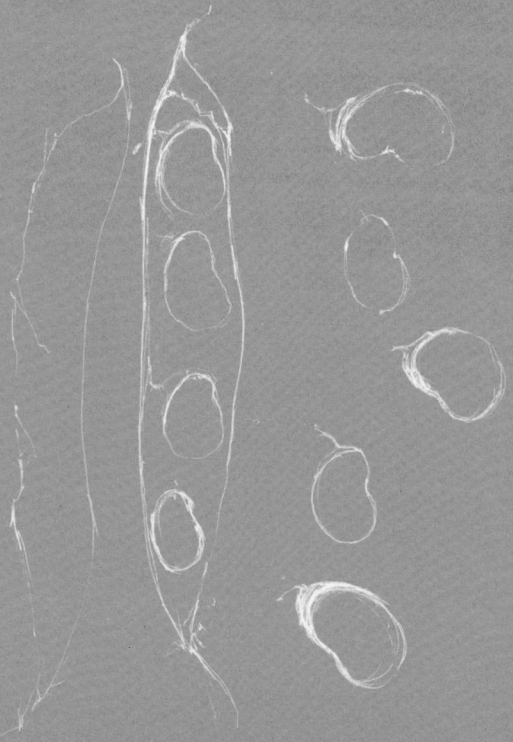

JUNE | JULY | AUGUST

Courgette and goat's cheese tart with beetroot, watercress, and broad bean salad

"I have to come clean and say I'm completely in love with broad beans – and when they're with mint – well, I would gladly run away and elope. It's such a lovely, fresh combination and adding the beetroot and watercress gives it such a depth of colour and a zingy flavour, I don't think you can beat it as a summer dish". Simon MacDonnell

HANDS-ON TIME: 40 MINUTES PLUS 40 MINUTES CHILLING
COOKING TIME: 40 MINUTES
SERVES 6–8

FOR THE PASTRY
175g plain flour
100g cold butter
1 egg yolk
Very cold water to mix

FOR THE FILLING
2 medium free-range organic eggs plus 2 egg yolks
300ml double cream
100ml crème fraîche
1tbsp olive oil
2 small courgettes, trimmed and sliced into thin discs
75g Cerney goat's cheese (delicious, creamy and fresh goat's cheese from the Cotswolds) or other soft goat's cheese, crumbled
25g pine nuts

FOR THE SALAD
3 whole beetroot, roasted, peeled and sliced
2 bunches watercress
200g broad beans (podded and blanched)
1/2 bunch mint, roughly chopped

Preheat the oven to 180°C (350°F) Gas mark 4.

Sift the flour into a large bowl with a pinch of salt.

Rub in the butter until the mixture resembles coarse breadcrumbs. Add the egg yolk and 1-2tbsp water to the mixture. Mix to a firm dough, first with a knife, and finally with your hand. You might need to add a drop more water but do so sparingly. Even though crumbly pastry is more difficult to handle, it produces a shorter, lighter result.

Chill, wrapped, in the fridge for 30 minutes before using. Lightly dust the work surface with flour. Roll out the pastry with a lightly floured rolling pin to around 1cm thick. Drape the pastry over a rolling pin and carefully lift over a 23cm tart tin. Ease the pastry into the corners using the side of your finger. Roll the rolling pin across the top edge of the tart tin to remove any excess pastry. Chill until firm while you prepare the filling. To bake, preheat the oven to 200°C (400°F) gas mark 6. Line the pastry case with a sheet of greaseproof paper and fill with baking beans. Bake until the sides of the pastry case are just cooked (around 15 minutes) then remove the beans and paper and return to the oven for a further few minutes until the base is done.

To make the filling, put the whole eggs in a bowl and whisk together with the egg yolks, cream and crème fraîche. Season to taste with salt and black pepper.

Heat 1tbsp oil in small pan and add the sliced courgettes, cook over a medium heat until softened and starting to colour. Add to the egg mixture.

Carefully pour the egg and courgette mixture into the pastry case and crumble over the goat's cheese. Bake in the oven for 25 minutes until just golden and set with a light wobble in the centre. Ten minutes before the end of cooking time, remove carefully from the oven and sprinkle over the pine nuts.

To make the salad, mix the cooked, cooled and sliced beetroot with the watercress, broad beans and chopped mint. Make a hazelnut vinaigrette using 1tbsp hazelnut oil, 2tbsp groundnut oil and 1tbsp sherry vinegar. Mix together well, pour over the salad and toss well to coat.

Serve the tart and salad together on a hot, sunny day.

JUNE | JULY | AUGUST

Gazpacho

By Stuart Seth

HANDS-ON TIME: 20 MINUTES PLUS 1 HOUR CHILLING
SERVES 6-8

7 vine tomatoes
1/2 cucumber peeled, de-seeded and roughly chopped
1 small red onion, peeled and finely chopped
1 red chilli, de-seeded and chopped
4 garlic cloves, peeled and chopped
1 red pepper, de-seeded and chopped
500ml carton tomato juice
Splash sherry vinegar
1 cup olive oil, plus extra to serve
Handful breadcrumbs

Put all the ingredients in a blender. Whiz together until smooth and blended. Transfer to a jug or bowl and chill in the fridge for 1 hour or until ready to serve. Serve chilled with a splash of extra virgin olive oil on the top

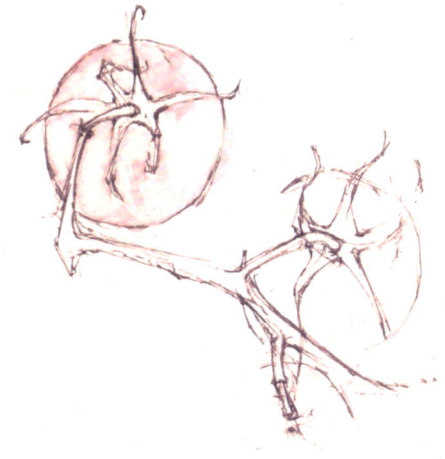

JUNE | JULY | AUGUST

Baked sea bream, as in the Balearics

"This is a wonderfully simple dish which is great to serve up in the middle of the table in the roasting dish. The sweet roasted flavours combine beautifully with a really fresh whole fish making it a great one-pot summer meal". Mitchell Tonks

HANDS-ON TIME: 15 MINUTES
COOKING TIME: 25 MINUTES
SERVES 2

2 potatoes, peeled and sliced into rounds about 1cm thick
One 450g sea bream, scaled and gutted
2 tomatoes, quartered
2 garlic cloves, peeled
Pinch sugar
Good-quality olive oil
Small handful fresh breadcrumbs
Small handful parsley, finely chopped
Lemon wedges, to serve

Preheat the oven to its highest setting.

Parboil the sliced potatoes in plenty of boiling, salted water for 3-4 minutes. Put the whole fish in a roasting tin and season with salt.

Arrange the potatoes, tomatoes and whole garlic cloves around the fish.

Sprinkle over a pinch each of sugar and salt. Pour in a few good glugs of olive oil and scatter over the breadcrumbs. Cover the tin tightly with foil and bake in the preheated oven for 20 minutes. Remove from the oven and sprinkle over the chopped parsley. Bake, uncovered for a further 5 minutes. Serve with lemon wedges to squeeze over.

Mitchell Tonks is a restaurateur, food writer and chef. He owns The Seahorse restaurant in Dartmouth. www.seahorserestaurant.co.uk

JUNE | JULY | AUGUST

Simple rosewater cake

"This easy cake with its slightly crunchy glaze is lovely by itself for tea, or with summer fruits for pudding. It's pretty decorated with fresh scented rose petals from the garden (choose ones which haven't been sprayed). Frost them if you have time, by brushing each petal on both sides with beaten egg white, and dipping it in caster sugar. Leave to dry on baking parchment before scattering over the cake". Xanthe Clay

HANDS-ON TIME: 20 MINUTES
COOKING TIME: 35–40 MINUTES

170g butter
170g caster sugar
3 eggs
225g self raising flour
6tbsp rosewater
225g icing sugar
1tbsp lemon juice

cook's tip

The best rosewaters can be found in Middle Eastern grocers and some delis. Don't use rosewater BP from the chemist: it has bitter compounds added to make it inedible.

Preheat the oven to 180°C (350°F) Gas mark 4. Grease and base line a 20cm x 25cm square cake tin.

Cream together the butter and sugar until light, then beat in the eggs one at a time. Mix in the flour, then 4tbsp rosewater. Turn into the tin, level the surface with a spatula and bake for 35 – 40 minutes.

Leave the cake to cool in the tin while you mix together the icing sugar, remaining 2tbsp rosewater and lemon juice to make a glaze. Prick the still warm cake all over with a fork and pour over the glaze. Leave to cool completely then remove from the tin and cut into squares or fingers.

Xanthe Clay writes for several major newspapers and magazines. Her book Recipes to Know by Heart is published in September 2008 by Mitchell Beazley

For Every Season | 37

JUNE | JULY | AUGUST

Lamb, olive and aubergine stew

"I can't resist the combination of lamb and aubergines. Stews aren't generally good in hot weather but this one is". Fiona Beckett

HANDS-ON TIME: 20 MINUTES
COOKING TIME: AROUND 2 HRS
SERVES 4–6

4-5tbsp olive oil
750g shoulder of lamb, fat trimmed and cubed
1 medium sized aubergine, cubed
1 medium onion, peeled and sliced
2 large garlic cloves, crushed
400g very ripe tomatoes, skinned and roughly chopped or
400g can chopped tomatoes
1/2tsp cinnamon
1tsp ground cumin
115g black olives marinated with garlic and herbs
2 heaped tbsp flat-leafed parsley or coriander, chopped

Heat half the oil in a large frying pan or casserole dish. Add the lamb to the pan and cook briefly on all sides until brown. You may have to do this in two batches.

Transfer the meat to a plate with a slotted spoon. Tip the aubergine into the pan and stir-fry over a medium-high heat until it starts to brown. If the aubergine starts to catch, add a little extra oil. Remove from the pan and set aside.

Reduce the heat, add the remaining oil and fry the onion for about 3-4min until it starts to soften. Add the crushed garlic and chopped tomatoes and cook for a further 3-4 minutes until the tomatoes break down and become jammy. Stir in the cinnamon, cumin and olives and pour in a small glass (about 125ml) of water. Return the meat to the pan, stir and bring to the boil. Reduce the heat to low, cover and simmer for 1 ½ hrs until the meat is tender, stirring occasionally. Add a little extra water if it starts to dry out. Season to taste with salt and black pepper and stir in the chopped parsley or coriander. Serve with couscous and courgettes or a green salad.

JUNE | JULY | AUGUST

Summer fruit salad with sweet geranium leaves

"Sweet geranium (Pelargonium Graveolens) and many other varieties of scented geraniums are ever present on our windowsills here at Ballymaloe. We use the delicious lemon-scented leaves in all sorts of ways, occasionally we use the pretty purple flowers also to enliven and add magic to otherwise simple dishes. The crystallised leaves, all frosty and crinkly are wonderful with fresh cream cheese and fat, juicy blackberries. I discovered this recipe which has now become a perennial favourite quite by accident a few summers ago as I raced to make a pudding in a hurry with the ingredients I had at that moment". Darina Allen

HANDS-ON TIME: 5 MINUTES
COOKING TIME: 5 MINUTES PLUS 3-4 HOURS MACERATING
SERVES 8–10

110g raspberries
110g loganberries
110g redcurrants
110g blackcurrants
110g small strawberries
110g blueberries
110g fraises du bois or wild strawberries
110g blackberries

FOR THE SYRUP
400g sugar
450ml water
6-8 large sweet geranium leaves

Put all the freshly picked berries into a white china or glass bowl.

Put the sugar, water and sweet geranium leaves into a stainless steel pan and bring slowly to the boil, stirring until the sugar dissolves. Boil for just 2 minutes. Cool for 4-5 minutes then pour the hot syrup over the fruit and leave to macerate for several hours.

Remove the geranium leaves. Serve the fruit salad chilled on its own or with softly whipped cream or vanilla ice-cream. Just before serving, scatter over a few fresh sweet geranium leaves

SUMMER BERRY JELLY WITH SWEET GERANIUM LEAVES
Sometimes when we have a berry salad left over, particularly if there's more juice than fruit we make it into a jelly. Use 4tsp gelatine for every 570ml of liquid. You'll need 1.2l liquid to fill a large ring mould. Once the jelly has set, turn out carefully onto a large white china plate, fill the centre with softly whipped cream and decorate with geranium leaves.

WINTER FRUIT SALAD
Follow the recipe for Summer Fruit Salad but substitute best quality frozen and thawed berries and currants

Ireland's best-loved cook and food writer, Darina Allen also runs Ballymaloe Cookery School, Ballymaloe, Shanagarry, Co. Cork, Ireland www.cookingisfun.ie

JUNE | JULY | AUGUST

Stuffed summer vegetables

"Many vegetables – cabbages, pumpkin or squashes, onions, potatoes, courgettes or aubergines – can be stuffed, but peppers and tomatoes make the most natural containers. You can vary the filling: if you are a meat eater, try minced meat instead of the rice". Jeanette Orrey

HANDS-ON TIME: 20 MINUTES
COOKING TIME: 50 MINUTES
SERVES 4

4 large peppers, or 4 beef tomatoes
4tbsp olive oil
225g onions, peeled and finely chopped
1 garlic clove, peeled and crushed
2tbsp pine nuts
85g long-grain rice
3tbsp finely chopped parsley
1tbsp finely chopped fresh dill
225ml water
400g can chopped tomatoes
1tsp mixed dried herbs

Preheat the oven to 180°C (350°F) Gas mark 4. Cut a lid off the top of each pepper and scoop out the cores and seeds. Do the same with the tomatoes if using and leave them to drain upside down for a while. Reserve the lids. Put in an oiled ovenproof dish.

To make the stuffing, heat 2tbsp oil in a medium pan and fry the onion and garlic until softened and lightly coloured. Add the pine nuts, rice, herbs and water, and cook gently for 10 minutes.

Stuff the rice mixture into the hollowed out peppers or tomatoes to about three-quarters full (the rice will swell as it cooks). Replace the lids and drizzle with the remaining olive oil. Mix together the chopped tomatoes and herbs. Pour around the stuffed vegetables and add a little water. Bake in the preheated oven for about 40 minutes until the vegetables are tender but still hold their shape.

Sieve or liquidise the tomato sauce, if you like, before serving with the vegetables.

For Every Season

JUNE | JULY | AUGUST

Sweet and sour shrimp and pineapple soup

By Prue Leith

HANDS-ON TIME: 25 MINUTES
COOKING TIME: AROUND 10 MINUTES
SERVES 4

2 small tomatoes, preferably slightly unripe
1 small pineapple, preferably slightly unripe
2 star fruit, preferably slightly unripe
3 spring onions, including green parts
1kg raw king prawns or langoustines
Large handful fresh coriander leaves
1 fresh long red chilli
2-3tbsp vegetable oil
2tbsp fish sauce (Nam Pla)
2tbsp lemon juice
1/2tsp ground pepper
2tbsp tamarind puree, optional
1-2tsp sugar (to taste)
250ml weak fish or vegetable stock

serving suggestion
Traditional accompaniments to this recipe are steamed rice and more herbs like Thai basil, coriander and spinach

Peel and quarter the tomatoes. Peel, core and chop the pineapple into chunks.

Thinly slice the star fruit and spring onions, shell the raw prawns or langoustine, roughly chop the coriander, de-seed and thinly slice the chilli.

Heat the oil in a large pan. Add half the tomatoes and cook for about 3 minutes just until they become watery.

Add fish sauce, pineapple, star fruit, lemon juice, pepper, tamarind, if using and sugar to taste.

Add the stock, sliced spring onions and remaining tomatoes then bring to the boil and bubble for 2 minutes. Add the prawns and cook for a further minute. Remove the pan from the heat, stir in the chopped coriander and chilli slices and serve immediately.

Founder of Leith's Good Food Group, Leith's Restaurant and Leith's School of Food and Wine, Prue Leith OBE is now the Chair of the School Food Trust, charged with improving school dinners. www.schoolfoodtrust.org.uk

JUNE | JULY | AUGUST

Steamed mussels with tomato and tarragon

By Rick Stein

HANDS-ON TIME: 10 MINUTES
COOKING TIME: AROUND 10 MINUTES
SERVES 2

1kg mussels
30ml extra virgin olive oil
2 garlic cloves, peeled and finely chopped
30ml dry white wine
30g unsalted butter
55g tomatoes, peeled, de-seeded and finely chopped
5g French tarragon, finely chopped

Make sure the mussels are tightly closed. Throw away any that are broken or that stay open when tapped sharply on a surface. If the mussels show any signs of grit or sand, wash them in plenty of cold water.

Heat the olive oil in a large pan. Add the chopped garlic and cook gently for around a minute to soften. Add the mussels to the pan and turn up the heat. Pour in the white wine, cover with a lid and cook for a few minutes, stirring once or twice until all the shells are just opened. Remove from the heat and drain into a colander set over a bowl to catch the cooking liquor.

Set the mussels aside to keep warm and transfer the reserved liquor to a pan. Bring to the boil then whisk in the butter followed by the chopped tomatoes and tarragon. Taste to check the seasoning. It's a good idea to leave seasoning to the end with shellfish because you never know how salty they are. Return the mussels to the pan. Serve with plenty of crusty bread or alternatively with a mound of linguine, cooked until just 'al dente'.

JUNE | JULY | AUGUST

Baked peaches

"We've said it many times before: the perfect dessert after a rich and satisfying meal is a perfect piece of fruit, and the most perfect fruit has to be a perfect peach. Its texture is luscious, its aroma is intoxicating, its flavour ravishing, and its juice runs everywhere".

Alice Waters

HANDS-ON TIME: 10 MINUTES
COOKING TIME: 30–45 MINUTES
SERVES 4

4 large ripe peaches
5tbsp apricot jam
2tbsp honey
225ml water
1tbsp lemon zest
2tsp fresh lemon juice
Caster sugar

Preheat oven to 200°C (400°F) gas mark 6. Halve the peaches and remove the stones. Put the peach halves cut-side up in a shallow earthenware baking dish measuring 23cm x 35cm.

In a small bowl, whisk together the jam, honey, water, lemon zest and juice. Spoon the mixture over the peach halves and sprinkle each half with 1/2 tsp sugar.

Bake for 30-45 minutes, until the peaches are tender. Very ripe peaches will cook faster. Check several times during baking, basting them with their juices each time you do. Serve warm with ice cream. Drizzle over the juices for a delicious sauce.

The Art of Simple Food by Alice Waters, Clarkson Potter
Chez Panisse Restaurant and Café, 1517 Shattuck Avenue, Berkeley, CA 94709-1516

For Every Season | 43

JUNE | JULY | AUGUST

Assiette de crudités Maman Blanc

"This is one of my favourite starters. My father would grow these vegetables and my mother would place them on the table on Sunday - the simplest, purest transition from the earth to the table. Depending on the time of year, there is a whole host of other salads you can use; beans, lentils, fennel, artichokes or finely shredded cabbage". Raymond Blanc

HANDS-ON TIME: 30 MINUTES PLUS 30 MINUTES MARINATING;
SERVES 4 – 6

- 400g beetroot, cooked peeled and sliced
- 4 banana shallots, finely chopped
- 150g cucumber, peeled and finely sliced
- 150g potato, diced into 1cm cubes, cooked for 5-6 minutes
- 200ml mayonnaise
- 15g flat-leafed parsley, chopped
- 150g French beans, topped and tailed, blanched and refreshed in iced water and drained
- 300g celeriac, peeled, grated and mixed with 2tbsp lemon juice
- 240g carrots, peeled and grated
- 4 free-range, organic eggs, boiled for 10 minutes, refreshed, peeled and quartered
- 400g Roma plum, vine ripened tomatoes, finely sliced

FOR THE VINAIGRETTE
- 180ml groundnut oil (or other non scented oil)
- 45ml white wine vinegar

First make the vinaigrette. Mix together the oil and vinegar and season with salt and black pepper. Mix the cooked sliced beetroot with 2tbsp of the vinaigrette and a quarter of the chopped shallots. Season with salt and black pepper and set aside. Sprinkle a pinch of salt over the sliced cucumber and leave to marinate for 30 minutes. Rinse and drain.

Mix the cooked diced potato with 2tbsp of the mayonnaise, 1/3 of the remaining chopped shallot and 1/4 of the chopped parsley. Season with salt and black pepper. Set aside.

Add the remaining chopped shallot with 2tbsp vinaigrette to the cooked French beans, season with salt and black pepper and set aside.

Mix the sliced cucumber with 1tbsp vinaigrette and adjust the seasoning with salt. Mix the grated celeriac with 2tbsp mayonnaise and season with salt and black pepper. For the grated carrot, add 2tbsp vinaigrette and season with salt and black pepper.

To serve, arrange the different salads, eggs and sliced tomatoes on a large serving platter with the remaining mayonnaise on the side.

cook's tip
The success of this simple dish relies on the freshest produce from your garden or farmers' market. Grate the celeriac thickly to give the shreds a good texture and the carrots slightly thinner than the celeriac if possible.

JUNE | JULY | AUGUST

Rosehip, cava and raspberry trifle

"This delicious autumn trifle is aromatic and rich but nice and light. You will need six trifle glasses or ramekins plus some specialist ingredients". Mark Evans

HANDS-ON TIME: AROUND 10 MINUTES
COOKING TIME: AROUND 25 MINUTES PLUS 1HR CHILLING; SERVES 4

200g raspberries
325ml cava, preferably organic (drink the rest once opened!)
Juice of 1 lemon
3 kaffir lime leaves, dried or fresh
55ml rosehip syrup (or 30g dried rosehip with 4tbsp caster sugar)
2tbsp agar agar flakes
Handful macadamia nuts, roughly crushed plus 500ml tub Yeo Valley Greek yoghurt with honey to serve

Carefully rinse and gently shake the raspberries to dry (this is important as soggy raspberries will inhibit the setting process). Divide the fruit between four glasses or ramekins.

Put the cava in a small, stainless steel pan with the lemon juice, lime leaves and rosehip syrup (or dried rosehip and sugar) and 200ml water. Bring the mixture gently to the boil. Simmer for 12 minutes to infuse and cook out the alcohol from the cava.

Strain the liquid into a measuring jug then return to a clean stainless steel pan. Add 1 heaped tbsp agar agar flakes for every 275ml liquid and whisk gently to help the flakes dissolve.

Simmer gently for 10 – 12 minutes, whisking gently from time to time. Strain the pale red liquid through a fine sieve into a jug. If you find crystals left at the bottom of the pan, the agar agar has not completely dissolved. Return the liquid to the pan, add another 1tbsp agar agar and simmer for a further few minutes, whisking gently, until completely dissolved.

Leave to cool in a jug for 2 minutes then divide the liquid among the glasses or ramekins of raspberries and chill in the fridge for 1 hour.

Serve, topped with crushed macadamia nuts and a good blob of Greek yoghurt with honey.

cook's tip
Agar agar is a vegetarian alternative to gelatine. You can find it along with rosehip syrup in good health food shops.

JUNE | JULY | AUGUST

Fresh rhubarb and orange relish

"This sweet, sour and mildly spiced relish is quick to make, and goes equally well with grilled mackerel or a fine pork pie. Coal black kalonji seeds are also known as black onion seeds and have a nutty flavour. They are usually available from well-stocked spice shelves of delis and larger supermarkets, but if you can't find any, black mustard seeds make a good alternative".

Sophie Grigson

HANDS-ON TIME: 15 MINUTES
COOKING TIME: AROUND 35 MINUTES
SERVES 4 – 6

1 orange
1tsp kalonji seeds or black mustard seeds
75g caster sugar
1 heaped tsp coriander seed, coarsely crushed
1 level tsp caraway seeds, coarsely crushed
2 stems rhubarb (about 250g), cut into matchsticks
A pinch or two of salt

cook's tip
Choose the reddest stems of rhubarb for the relish, to give it a rosy tint. Cutting the rhubarb into matchsticks (i.e. about 3.5cm long and 1/2cm thick) means that it cooks in a matter of minutes.

Pare the zest from the orange and cut into long thin shreds. Simmer in a pan of water for 5 minutes to remove any bitterness. Drain thoroughly. Squeeze the juice of the orange. Reserve a good pinch of the kalonji seeds or black mustard seeds.

Stir the orange juice, sugar, remaining spices and 2 tbsp water in a small pan over a medium heat until the sugar has dissolved. Bring up to the boil and add the orange zest. Simmer for 10 minutes until the liquid is very thick and syrupy. If absolutely necessary, add a little more water. If the syrup is still rather watery boil hard for a couple of minutes.

Now add the rhubarb and salt and stir. Cover and cook for 1 minute to get the juices flowing, then take off the lid and cook for another 2 minutes, stirring once.

Take off the heat, then use a slotted spoon to lift out the rhubarb and orange zest, leaving as much of the juice behind as possible. Transfer the rhubarb and orange zest to a pretty serving bowl.

Return the pan to a high heat, and boil hard until very thick and no more than a sticky layer barely covering the base of the pan. Pour this reduced mixture over the rhubarb and stir, then leave to cool. Sprinkle with the reserved kalonji seeds or mustard seeds before serving.

JUNE | JULY | AUGUST

Garden salad of almost raw vegetables with goat's cheese

"This is a salad of thinly sliced summer vegetables. You could use radishes or kohlrabi or mouli or turnip or any other root vegetable. Cauliflower, broken into tiny florets is good too. The vegetables need to be fresh, firm and crunchy. Keep the beetroot separate until the last minute so that it doesn't stain the other vegetables". Barny Haughton

HANDS-ON TIME: 20 MINUTES
SERVES 4

Juice of a lemon
White wine vinegar
Extra virgin olive oil
2 courgettes
2 carrots, peeled
1 bulb fennel
4 baby beetroot, scrubbed
Handful of freshly podded peas or broad beans, blanched
Large handful of peppery salad leaves (rocket, watercress, mustard leaves etc)
Small bunch mint or basil or tarragon or marjoram
350g soft crumbly goat's cheese (but good feta will do nicely), optional but lovely

In a big salad bowl, make a dressing with one part lemon juice (plus a splash of white vinegar and 1/2tsp salt) to four parts of olive oil. Pour a little of this dressing into a smaller bowl to reserve for the beetroot.

Using a very sharp knife or mandolin, slice the courgettes, carrots and fennel into thin ribbon lengths. Transfer to the large bowl. Slice the beetroot and transfer to the smaller bowl. Toss the vegetables in the dressing, then add the blanched peas or beans, salad leaves and mint and toss gently together. Arrange the beetroot prettily on the salad, crumble over the cheese, if using and serve.

Serve with baked potatoes or plain rice or just good bread

cook's tip

To blanch vegetables, bring a suitably-sized pan of water to the boil. Add the prepared vegetables and cook until they are just tender but still retain a bite. To refresh, transfer the vegetables from the pan to a bowl of iced water to stop the cooking process and to ensure the vegetables keep their colour and texture.

Barny Haughton is chef-proprietor of Bordeaux Quay, V-Shed, Canons Way, Bristol, BS1 5UH www.bordeaux-quay.co.uk

JUNE | JULY | AUGUST

Sparkling summer cherry jelly

"This year I launched CherryAid, a campaign to save the British cherry. You can be sure this recipe will be part of National Cherry Day's celebratory feast". Henrietta Green

HANDS-ON TIME: 15 MINUTES PLUS 1–2 HOURS CHILLING
COOKING TIME: 10 MINUTES
SERVES 4

5 gelatine leaves
500ml sparkling white wine or Prosecco
200g caster sugar
Handful of mint leaves, lightly crushed
Almond oil for greasing
450g black cherries such as Bradbourne Blacks, stoned and halved

Put the gelatine leaves in a bowl, cover with cold water and leave to soak until softened. Meanwhile pour the sparkling wine into a saucepan, add the sugar and mint and simmer gently over a low heat until the sugar has dissolved. Remove from the heat and strain off the mint leaves. Squeeze the softened leaves of gelatine with your hands to get rid of the excess liquid, add immediately to the warm wine syrup, stir briefly and leave to cool for a short time but not long enough that it starts to set. Strain and decant into a jug.

Lightly oil four 200ml individual jelly moulds – dariole moulds or even cups will do. Arrange a layer of cherries on the bottom of each mould, carefully pour over a little wine mixture just enough to cover the fruit, and leave to set in the fridge for no more than a few minutes or until it starts to set at the outside edges. Repeat the process with the cherries and wine until the moulds are full, then leave to set firmly in the fridge for 1-2 hours. If the wine mixture begins to set before you've finished, just warm it gently so that it is liquid enough to pour over the fruit.

To turn the jellies out of their moulds, dip them briefly in hot water, lay a serving plate on top of each, turn it over and give the mould a short sharp shake. The jelly should just slip out; if not, try loosening it around the edges with a sharp knife. Decorate the jellies with a couple of whole cherries and dust with icing sugar.

JUNE | JULY | AUGUST

Roasted garlic and parsley fish stew

"This is a very simple dish that can be cooked in one pot. If the fish suggested are unavailable or out of season you can use hake, gurnard or haddock (smoked or natural) in their place".

Dave Daly

HANDS-ON TIME: 30 MINUTES
COOKING TIME: AROUND 40 MINUTES
SERVES 4

1 head garlic
3 medium waxy potatoes, peeled and chopped into 1-2cm cubes
Olive oil
6 shallots, finely diced
2 bulbs fennel, diced into 1cm cubes
50ml white wine
150ml fish stock
300-400g salmon fillet (skin-on) cut into 8 pieces
300-400g grey mullet fillets (skin-on) cut into 8 pieces
50ml double cream
250g mussels, de-bearded
Bunch flat-leafed parsley, picked and chopped

Preheat the oven to 180°C (350°F) gas mark 4. Wrap the garlic in foil and roast in the oven for 20 minutes or until soft. Set aside until needed.

Cook the potatoes in plenty of boiling, salted water until just tender. Drain well and set aside

Heat 2tbsp olive oil in a medium pan over a gentle heat. Add the diced shallot and fennel and cook until softened but not coloured.

Squeeze the softened garlic out its papery casings and into the pan. Pour in the wine and bring to the boil then turn down the heat to a simmer and bubble until the liquid is reduced by two thirds. Add the fish stock and return to the boil. Reduce the heat to a simmer and add the salmon and mullet pieces to the pan

When the fish starts to flake, remove from the liquor with a slotted spoon and set aside to keep warm. Add the cream and boil gently for 4-5 minutes. Add the mussels, potato and most of the parsley and gently simmer until the mussels have opened. Season to taste with salt. Divide between four warmed bowls, sprinkle over the remaining parsley and serve with crusty bread.

Dave Daly is senior sous-chef at Bordeaux Quay, V-Shed, Canons Way, Bristol, BS1 5UH www.bordeaux-quay.co.uk

FOR Every Season 49

JUNE | JULY | AUGUST

And another thing...

Raspberries and cream

Break up meringues, roughly crush raspberries and softly whip some double cream (stop just before you think it's ready as it'll overwhip in a second). Add the fruit and all its juices to the cream with the meringue shards. Fold briefly together and serve for the easiest summer pudding.

Broad beans

Cook 250g baby broad beans in boiling salted water for 2 minutes then drain. Fry 100g salami or chorizo in a hot pan until the fat starts to run and the salami begins to crisp. Add the broad beans to the pan and toss together. Serve with crusty bread.

Globe artichokes

Whole à la vinaigrette, or cooked in the Roman manner with olive oil, garlic and lemon and served as an accompaniment to simply roasted lamb or veal, globe artichokes are one of the less well known but wonderful products of this season.

Autumn

Swede, sweetcorn, kale, fennel, squash, wild mushrooms, salsify, celeriac, broccoli, chicory, endive, turnips, carrots, parsnips, apples, pears, chestnuts, quinces.......

And game. Try roast pheasant or mallard or pigeon with a roughly mashed, buttery nutmeg-seasoned mix of swede, carrot and celeriac.

SEPTEMBER | OCTOBER | NOVEMBER

Poached pears in cider

"With their hard greenish-brown skin, Conference pears never look very appealing but they have a superb flavour and are wonderful for poaching. You can do this just as successfully in cider as in red wine. A great dessert for when you've had an indulgent carb-laden main course like a pie!". Fiona Beckett

HANDS-ON TIME: 10 MINUTES
COOKING TIME: 1 HOUR 10 MINUTES
SERVES 4

4 evenly sized, under-ripe Conference pears
330ml can medium-dry cider
4-5 heaped tbsp golden caster sugar
Strip pared lemon rind
Small cinnamon stick
Lemon juice to taste
Pouring cream or vanilla ice cream, to serve

Carefully peel the pears with a small sharp knife, keeping them whole and leaving the stalk intact. Fit, side by side, into a medium-sized pan and pour over the cider. Add enough water to the pan to just cover the pears then remove the pears from the liquid and set aside.

Add 4 heaped tbsp of golden caster sugar to the pan and heat gently until dissolved. Taste the liquid and add a little extra sugar if you think it needs it (ciders vary).

Return the pears to the pan along with the pared lemon rind and cinnamon stick and bring to the boil. Reduce the heat, cover the pan and simmer for around 45 minutes until the pears are soft but not mushy.

Remove the pears carefully from the pan using a slotted spoon and transfer to a shallow glass dish. Remove the pared lemon rind and cinnamon stick then increase the heat and bubble the remaining liquid until thick, syrupy and reduced by about two thirds.

Taste the liquid and add a little lemon juice if necessary. Pour the syrup over the pears and leave to cool. Serve just warm or at room temperature with double cream or vanilla ice cream and some crisp home-baked biscuits or shortbread

cook's tip
Choose pears that aren't rock hard but not quite ripe enough to eat

SEPTEMBER | OCTOBER | NOVEMBER

Sweetcorn and brown shrimp fritters

By Sophie Grigson

HANDS-ON TIME: 10 MINUTES
COOKING TIME: AROUND 20 MINUTES
SERVES 6

125g plain flour
1/4 tsp salt
1tbsp sunflower or vegetable oil
1 egg, separated
150ml good quality lager or dry cider
Kernels from 2 sweetcorn cobs
150g peeled brown shrimp, or larger prawns, roughly chopped
oil for deep frying
Lemon wedges, cayenne pepper and chilli sauce, to serve

Tip the flour and salt into a mixing bowl. Make a well in the centre and add the oil, egg yolk and the lager or cider.

Gradually whisk the liquid into the flour, adding enough water (approximately 200-300ml) to form a batter with the consistency of runny double cream. Stir in the sweetcorn kernels and shrimps and set aside.

Shortly before serving, fill a frying pan to a depth of 2-3cm with oil and heat gently, or use an electric deep fat fryer. While the oil is heating, whisk the egg white until it forms stiff peaks, and gently fold into the sweetcorn and shrimp mixture. Drop a dessertspoon of mixture at a time into the hot oil and fry until golden brown underneath. Turn over and brown the other side, then lift out and drain on kitchen paper.

Serve swiftly with a squeeze or two of lemon and a dusting of cayenne or a shake of chilli sauce if you can take the heat.

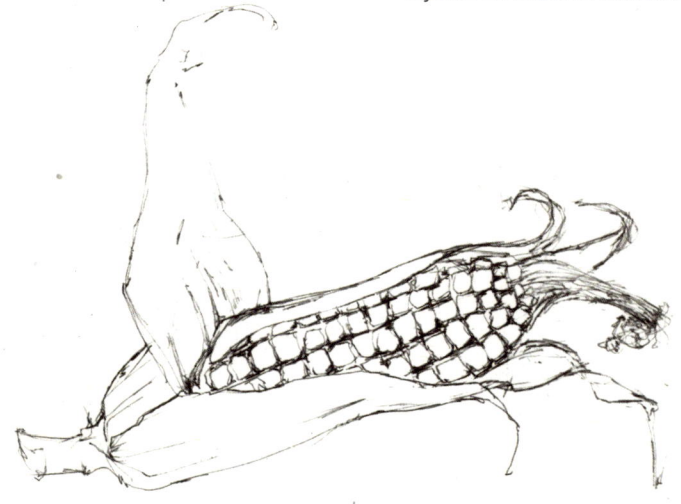

Sophie Grigson has written over 14 books to go with her many TV series. She has written columns and articles for numerous newspapers and magazines and was awarded the Guild of Food Writers Cookery Journalist Award in 2001. She is a regular feature at the Demo Kitchen at Bristol's Organic Food Festival

For Every Season | 53

SEPTEMBER | OCTOBER | NOVEMBER

Kidneys and bacon on toast with a little devilled sauce

"The perfect alternative to a Sunday morning fry-up". Gill Meller

HANDS-ON TIME: 10 MINUTES
COOKING TIME: 15 MINUTES
SERVES 2

100g unsmoked bacon or pancetta, chopped into smallish chunks
200g pig's kidneys, trimmed, halved and each half cut into three pieces
1tbsp cider vinegar
1/2 tbsp Worcester sauce
1tbsp sherry
1tsp English mustard
4 shakes of Tabasco or a pinch of cayenne pepper
1tbsp double cream
1tsp redcurrant or crab apple jelly
2tbsp finely chopped flat leaf parsley to serve

Heat a heavy-based frying pan over a medium-high heat. Add the bacon or pancetta and sizzle until the fat starts to run. Push the bacon to one side of the pan and throw in the kidneys. Sauté the kidneys for 1-2 minutes, until they begin to colour.

Increase the heat and add the vinegar, Worcester sauce and sherry to the pan and stir. Bubble until reduced by half and then add the mustard, Tabasco or cayenne, cream and redcurrant or crab apple jelly. Stir well to combine.

Bubble until the sauce is reduced and just thickened. Season to taste with salt and black pepper.

Spoon the kidneys and bacon over thick slices of hot toast with plenty of the rich sauce. Sprinkle over chopped parsley and serve immediately.

Gill Meller is head chef at River Cottage HQ, River Cottage, Park Farm, Trinity Hill, Axminster, Devon, EX13 5NX
www.rivercottage.net

SEPTEMBER | OCTOBER | NOVEMBER

Pasta with wild mushrooms and hare

"After a period of decline, hare populations in the UK are now stable. Conservation methods, like those employed on organic farms, are helping to protect this beautiful animal". Freddy Bird

HANDS-ON TIME: 30 MINUTES
COOKING TIME: AROUND 2 1/2 HOURS
SERVES 8

2tbsp olive oil
4 hare legs
200g fatty pork belly, bones removed and reserved, meat roughly chopped
2 glasses white wine
1 stick celery, finely chopped
1 large red onion, finely chopped
2 medium carrots, peeled and finely chopped
3 garlic cloves, peeled and finely chopped
around 600ml chicken stock
25g butter
100g wild or chestnut mushrooms, chopped
Few sprigs thyme, leaves removed and roughly chopped
800g fresh or dried pappardelle pasta

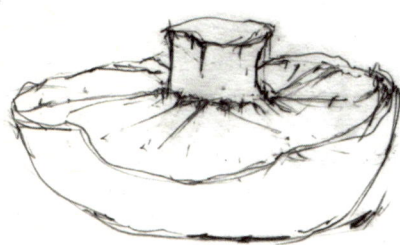

Heat the oil in a large frying pan or casserole. Add the hare legs and chopped pork belly and cook over a medium heat until golden on all sides. Deglaze the pan with the wine then add the celery, onion, carrots and garlic and cook over a medium heat, until softened and lightly browned.

Remove the pan from the heat and pour over enough stock to almost cover the hare legs. Loosely cover the ingredients with a cartouche (a damp piece of greaseproof paper, crumpled then flattened is all you need). Cover the pan again – this time with foil and cook over a very low heat for around 2 hours.

Lift out the hare and pork with a slotted spoon. Strain the cooking liquor through a sieve and discard the veg. Roughly shred the hare and pork. Return the cooking liquor to a pan and bring to the boil. Turn down the heat and simmer until reduced by a third.

Melt the butter in a frying pan and fry the mushrooms until softened. Mix together the mushrooms, shredded hare and pork, chopped thyme, reserved cooking liquor and a little more stock, if needed. The mixture should be moist but not wet. Season with salt and black pepper. Cook the pasta, gently warm the hare mixture in a pan and stir together. Serve immediately.

Freddy Bird is senior sous-chef at Bordeaux Quay, V-Shed, Canons Way, Bristol, BS1 5UH www.bordeaux-quay.co.uk

SEPTEMBER | OCTOBER | NOVEMBER

Pumpkin curry with crispy plantain chips

"This is a creamy West Indian-style mild curry, topped with crispy plantain chips, perfect to make in the autumn". Rachel Demuth

HANDS-ON TIME: 20 MINUTES
COOKING TIME: AROUND 40 MINUTES
SERVES 4

FOR THE CURRY
2tbsp sunflower oil
1 large onion, peeled and sliced
750g pumpkin, peeled, cut into large bite-sized pieces
A thumb-sized piece of fresh root ginger, peeled and finely chopped
2 garlic cloves, peeled and chopped
1tsp turmeric
1/4 tsp cayenne pepper
1/4 tsp ground cinnamon
1/2 tsp allspice
350ml coconut cream
100ml water
Juice of 1 lime
Juice of 1 orange
200g green beans, topped and tailed
4 large tomatoes, chopped into eighths
Handful of fresh coriander, chopped

FOR THE PLANTAIN CHIPS
2 ripe plantains
Sunflower oil for shallow frying
Chickpea or plain flour for dusting

Heat the oil in a large pan and fry the onion until softened.

Add the pumpkin, ginger and garlic and fry for 1 minute, stirring until fragrant but not browned.

Add the turmeric, cayenne, cinnamon, allspice and a pinch of salt. Cook, stirring for 30 seconds to warm the spices then add the coconut cream, water, lime and orange juice. Bring to the boil then simmer for 10 minutes. Add the green beans and tomatoes and simmer for a further 10 minutes until the vegetables are cooked through but still retain a bite.

Meanwhile, make the plantain chips. Peel and thickly slice the plantain on an angle into slices measuring 1/2cm thick.

Heat a little sunflower oil in a shallow frying pan, dust the slices with flour and fry gently until just blackened on both sides. Remove from the pan and sprinkle with a little salt.

Once the curry is cooked, season to taste with salt and black pepper. Scatter over plenty of chopped coriander and serve with steamed rice and a few fried plantain chips

cook's tip
Plantains are known as cooking bananas. They are larger than sweet bananas with thick tough skins. When they're still green and unripe, they are delicious used as a vegetable in curries. Ripe, yellow plantains work best for chips.

SEPTEMBER | OCTOBER | NOVEMBER

Cabbage with bacon

"I'm very happy to eat this simple dish by itself as a vegetable rich supper, but it's also very good with grilled or poached fish. Use whatever cured pork you like. Offcuts bought cheaply from the butcher, the stubby end of a chorizo, or any good leftover scraps are perfect". Xanthe Clay

HANDS ON TIME: 10 MINUTES
COOKING TIME: AROUND 30 MINUTES;
SERVES 4 AS A SIDE DISH,
2 AS A MAIN COURSE

Around 115g streaky bacon or pancetta or chorizo, chopped
1 onion, peeled and chopped
1 savoy cabbage, sliced (include some of the dark green leaves)

Heat a large pan over a medium heat. Add the bacon and cook until the fat starts to run, adding a little olive oil or dripping if it is lean.

Add the chopped onion with a little salt and pepper and cook gently until softened and translucent. Stir in the sliced cabbage and cover with a lid.

Cook until the cabbage begins to wilt, then uncover and continue cooking until soft but not soggy. Season with plenty of black pepper to taste and serve immediately.

Xanthe Clay writes for several major newspapers and magazines. Her book Recipes to Know by Heart is published in September 2008 by Mitchell Beazley

For Every Season

SEPTEMBER | OCTOBER | NOVEMBER

Six minute autumn raspberry jam

"This is the first recipe I show my students how to make to take the mystery out of jam making. It takes just 5 or 6 minutes to reach setting point (hence its name!). In fact, it is possible to make a batch of scones and in the time they take to bake, make this jam. Remember, you can make jam with even a single punnet of raspberries. Just use equal quantities of sugar to fruit. Once it's made, hide the jam in a cool place or store in your kitchen so you can feel great every time you look at it! Anyway, it's so delicious it won't last long!". Darina Allen

HANDS-ON TIME: 15 MINUTES
COOKING TIME: AROUND 20 MINUTES
MAKES 1.35KG

900g white sugar (use 225g less if fruit is very sweet)
900g fresh autumn raspberries

RASPBERRY AND CASSIS PRESERVE
Follow the recipe above. Stir in 4tbsp crème de cassis to the mixure just before potting

RASPBERRY AND BLACKBERRY JAM
Use 800g raspberries and 100g blackberries. Mix together and follow the recipe above

RASPBERRY AND LOGANBERRY JAM
Use 450g raspberries and 450g loganberries. Mix together and follow the recipe above

LOGANBERRY JAM
Substitute loganberries for raspberries and follow the recipe above.

TAYBERRY JAM
Tayberries are the delicious result of a blackberry and raspberry cross. The berries, developed in Scotland, appear to display the best qualities of both parents. They are named after the River Tay. Substitute tayberries for raspberries and follow the recipe above

cook's tip
To sterilise jam jars, preheat the oven to 120°C (250°F) gas mark 1/2. Wash the jars and lids in hot, soapy water. Rinse and leave to dry in the preheated oven for 10 minutes. Remove and fill with jam whilst still warm.

Preheat the oven to 180°C (350°F) gas mark 4. Tip the sugar onto a baking sheet and shake to cover the base evenly. Warm the sugar in the oven for 5-10 minutes.

Put the raspberries in a wide stainless steel pan and cook for 3-4 minutes until the juices begin to run. As soon as the mixture starts to bubble, add the hot sugar. Reduce the heat and stir until the sugar is fully dissolved.

Increase the heat and boil steadily for around 5 minutes, stirring frequently.

Test for a set by putting 1tsp jam on a chilled plate and leave for a few minutes in a cool place. It should wrinkle when pushed gently with a finger. Once the jam has reached setting point, remove from the heat, skim off any froth and pour into sterilised jam jars. (See cook's tip). Cover immediately and store in a cool place.

SEPTEMBER | OCTOBER | NOVEMBER

Wild mushroom and butter bean soup

"A stalwart of winter months, I often make this soup with dried mushrooms. In autumn, when fresh wild mushrooms are readily available and not too hideously expensive, I use them instead which means – obviously – you don't have to soak them first".

Henrietta Green

HANDS-ON TIME: 20 MINUTES PLUS 30 MINUTES SOAKING
COOKING TIME: 1HR 50 MINS MINUTES
SERVES 4

25g dried wild mushrooms
2tbsp olive oil
1 onion, peeled and sliced
2 garlic cloves, peeled and crushed
500g dried butter beans, soaked overnight in water
150ml carton of full fat Greek-style yoghurt
25g butter
Small handful flat-leafed parsley, chopped

If you're using dried mushrooms, put in a suitable bowl, pour over 300ml boiling water and leave to soak for about 30 minutes until quite soft.

Lift out the mushrooms using a slotted spoon and refresh in a clean bowl with just enough cold water to cover. Reserve the soaking liquor. If it looks particularly gritty strain through a muslin lined sieve, otherwise just leave it as a few particles won't do any harm, in fact they will probably increase the flavour of the soup.

Heat the olive oil in a large pan and add the onion. Cook gently for about 10 minutes, until softened. Add the garlic and the drained and rinsed butter beans and stir to coat in the oil.

Pour in 700ml water and the reserved soaking liquor and gently bring to the boil. Simmer for about 90 minutes until the butter beans are completely softened.

Using either a hand blender or food processor, whiz the soup until smooth. Return to the pan, stir in the yoghurt, adjust the seasoning and gently reheat. If you like your soup with a bit of texture, keep a few whole butter beans back before you purée the soup, then stir them in with the yoghurt.

Meanwhile, melt the butter in a suitable sauté pan. Squeeze the mushrooms with your hands until dry then roughly chop. Add the mushrooms to the pan and cook gently over a medium heat for 5 minutes until tender. Stir into the soup, adjust the seasoning and sprinkle over some chopped parsley just before serving.

Writer, broadcaster and consultant, Henrietta Green is the author of the Food Lovers Guide to Britain. www.foodloversbritain.com

For Every Season | 59

SEPTEMBER | OCTOBER | NOVEMBER

Apple and sweet geranium jelly

By Darina Allen

HANDS-ON TIME: 20 MINUTES PLUS 24 HRS DRAINING
COOKING TIME: 1 1/2 HOURS
MAKES AROUND 3KG

2.7kg crab apples or Bramley Seedlings, washed, quartered and any bruises cut out
6-8 large sweet geranium leaves (Pelargonium Graveolens) plus a few extra
2.7l water
Juice and pared rind of 2 unwaxed lemons, preferably organic
Granulated sugar

Put the apples in a large pan with the geranium leaves, water and lemon rind and cook over a low heat for around 1 hour until the apples dissolve into a mush.

Scoop into a jelly bag and leave to drip over a suitable container until all the juice has been extracted - usually overnight. Measure the juice into a preserving pan. For every 570ml juice, you will need 450g granulated sugar.

Preheat the oven to 180°C (350°F) gas mark 4. Tip the sugar onto a baking sheet and shake to cover the base evenly. Warm the sugar in the oven for 5-10 minutes.

Squeeze the lemons, strain the juice and add to the preserving pan. Taste the mixture and add a few more geranium leaves if the flavour is very mild. Bring to the boil and add the warmed sugar. Set the pan over a gentle heat and stir until the sugar is dissolved.

Increase the heat and boil rapidly without stirring for 8-10 minutes. Remove the geranium leaves with a slotted spoon. Test for a set by putting 1tsp jelly on a chilled plate and leave for a few minutes in a cool place. It should wrinkle when pushed gently with a finger. Once the jelly has reached setting point, remove from the heat, skim off any froth and pour into sterilised jam jars. Add a sweet geranium leaf to each jar of jelly then cover and seal immediately.

Ireland's best-loved cook and food writer, Darina Allen also runs Ballymaloe Cookery School, Ballymaloe, Shanagarry, Co. Cork, Ireland www.cookingisfun.ie

SEPTEMBER | OCTOBER | NOVEMBER

Pheasant casserole with ceps, pancetta and chestnuts

"For my 40th birthday, my Papadeli friends sent me on a foraging weekend in the Mendips. I found it absolutely fascinating learning about all the fabulous fungi out there in the countryside, right on our doorstep. What a great present – one I'll never forget and which has inspired me to use more mushrooms whenever I can! This recipe is one of my favourites – rich, velvety, flavoursome and warming – just what we need as the weather grows cooler and the leaves begin to fall". Simon MacDonnell

HANDS-ON TIME: 40 MINUTES
COOKING TIME: AROUND 4 HOURS
SERVES 4

FOR THE STOCK

2 pheasant carcasses
1 white onion, peeled and quartered
1 head celery, broken into sticks
2 carrots, peeled and halved
Small bunch thyme
A glass red wine

FOR THE CASSEROLE

2 large pheasants portioned into breast and leg pieces, carcasses reserved for stock (see above)
3tbsp olive oil
2 red onions, peeled and chopped
2 sticks celery, chopped
5 garlic cloves, peeled and finely chopped
1 bunch thyme
200g bacon or pancetta chopped
100g fresh or dried ceps, rehydrated in hot water for 20min, soaking liquor reserved
570ml red wine
100g cooked chestnuts

Preheat the oven to 180°C (350°F) gas mark 4.

To make the stock, put the carcasses in a roasting tin with the onion, celery sticks, halved carrots and thyme and roast for 20 minutes

Remove from the oven and add the red wine to the tin. Bring to the boil on the hob then carefully transfer the contents to a large pan with enough water to cover. Bring to the boil then reduce the heat and simmer gently for 2 hours, skimming occasionally.

Strain the stock, reserving the liquid.

To make the casserole, season the pheasant pieces with salt and pepper. Heat the olive oil in a medium heavy-based casserole, add the red onion, celery, garlic, thyme and bacon and cook over a low heat, stirring occasionally.

Add the ceps. Pour in the wine and bring to the boil. Add the reserved stock and strained cep liquor (if using dried ceps) and return to the boil. Add the pheasant pieces to the casserole. Cover the pan and cook for 40 minutes then add the chestnuts. Leave the casserole to cook over a low heat for a further 40 minutes. Remove the pheasant pieces from the sauce and keep warm. Continue cooking the sauce until it has reduced to a lovely velvety consistency, just as an autumnal stew should be! Serve with buttered greens and roasted root vegetables.

Simon MacDonnell owns and runs cafe and deli, Papadeli with his wife, Catrin. Papadeli, 84 Alma Road, Clifton, Bristol, BS8 2DJ www.papadeli.co.uk

SEPTEMBER | OCTOBER | NOVEMBER

Aligot

"Aligot is a Languedocien dish of mashed potato with cheese in it. Its origins go back to the medieval tradition of providing pilgrims on their way to Santiago de Compostela in Spain with cheap but sustaining and satisfying food. The best potatoes are the floury ones and since this is very much a winter rather than summer dish, suitable varieties - like Maris Piper, King Edward, Desirée & Pentland Javelin – will be at their best and readily available. The best – and authentic – cheese to use is Comté which you can get from good delis, but Gruyère is fine and a medium strong Cheddar will do too". Barny Haughton

HANDS-ON TIME: 30 MINUTES
COOKING TIME: 20 MINUTES
SERVES 8

1kg potatoes, peeled weight
50ml milk
50g butter
2 garlic cloves, peeled
400g Comté or other cheese, grated

Boil the potatoes in properly seasoned water (1tsp salt for every 1l of water) until well cooked but definitely not falling apart. Drain well and leave to cool in the colander for a few minutes. Return to the pan and mash well with the milk and butter. The mixture should be completely smooth. Meanwhile, put the garlic cloves on a chopping board, sprinkle over a little salt and use the flat of a large sharp knife to mash the garlic into a fine purée.

Return the mashed potato to a low heat, add the garlic purée, a pinch or two of white pepper and the cheese. Beat continuously until the mixture becomes stringy and elastic but still soft. Or until your arm hurts. You may need to add a little more milk. This will take about 10 minutes. (It should almost run off the spoon).

Serve with a good piece of roast beef or venison and some cabbage.

Barny Haughton is chef-proprietor of Bordeaux Quay, V-Shed, Canons Way, Bristol, BS1 5UH www.bordeaux-quay.co.uk

SEPTEMBER | OCTOBER | NOVEMBER

Lemon and thyme roast chicken

By Barny Haughton

HANDS-ON TIME: 20 MINUTES PLUS 20 MINUTES RESTING
COOKING TIME: AROUND 1 HOUR
SERVES 4–6

1 organic free-range chicken with giblets
2 garlic cloves, peeled
A small bunch thyme
1 lemon
100g unsalted butter, softened
Olive oil
1 glass white wine

An hour before cooking, remove the chicken from the fridge. Take the giblets out of the chicken and remove elastic or other trussing.

Preheat the oven to 200°C (400°F) gas mark 6. Crush the garlic cloves and chop the thyme leaves. Mix together with salt and black pepper.

Halve the lemon and stuff one half along with the garlic mixture into the cavity.

Gently ease the skin away from the breast of the chicken and insert the slightly softened butter into the space, distributing it smoothly and evenly. This is not as difficult as you think.

Rub olive oil over the whole skin surface of the bird. Season with salt and black pepper.

Put the bird on a roasting tray, pour in the wine and cook in the oven for 20 minutes. This is what Hugh Fearnley-Whittingstall calls the 20 minute sizzle. Remove the the chicken from the oven and baste well. Reduce the temperature to 170°C (325°F) gas mark 3. Cover the chicken with foil and return to the oven for a further 40 minutes or so. To check if the chicken is cooked, pierce the flesh between breast and thigh with the point of a knife. The juices should run clear.

Leave the chicken to rest in a warm place for 20 minutes. Remove the lemon and discard. Carve the chicken in the roasting tray, squeeze over the remaining half lemon and drizzle over olive oil. Serve.

cook's tip
You can make a lovely stock out of the carcass and neck and a salad or paté from the liver and heart.

Barny Haughton is chef-proprietor of Bordeaux Quay, V-Shed, Canons Way, Bristol, BS1 5UH www.bordeaux-quay.co.uk

For Every Season

SEPTEMBER | OCTOBER | NOVEMBER

Braised root vegetables

"A favourite vegetable that deserves more applause is the swede, the somewhat least of the root vegetables. It would seem the good name of the swede was tarnished in the same way as that of the innocent cabbage, both victims of scurrilous, woefully poor cooking. There is a curious fondness for these root vegetables in the Middle East and this recipe for braising the vegetables in olive oil, lemon and dill, I found years back in Claudia Roden`s Mediterranean Cookery. It is unusual and very good, doing wonders in filling a kitchen with a happy scent, and making abundant use of produce all too often just boiled and beaten with butter. Needless to say, we have corrupted the original recipe but not that much, I hope".

Jeremy Lee

HANDS-ON TIME: 20 MINUTES
COOKING TIME: AROUND 1 HOUR
SERVES 6 AS AN ACCOMPANIMENT

75ml good-quality olive oil
1 small onion, peeled and chopped
3 celery stalks, peeled and finely chopped
2 medium carrots
1/2 swede
3 turnips
1/2 small head celeriac
1 small parsnip
A great handful of fresh dill, chopped
1 lemon

Heat the oil in a wide, heavy bottomed pan. Tip in the onion and celery and cook until completely softened and uncoloured. Peel all the vegetables, taking care to ruthlessly remove any thicker peel from the larger vegetables that will toughen during cooking and diminish the final result.

Chop each vegetable into similar-sized pieces, (approximately 2.5cm square-ish) but they don't have to be the same shape, resembling more uncut mediaeval gemstones. Wash the vegetables well. Add the carrots to the pan first, cover and leave to cook gently for 5 minutes. Then add the swede and turnip and let that cook gently for a further 5 minutes. Once the pan is simmering lightly, add the rest of the vegetables and stir carefully but thoroughly. Add a little cup of water to aid the cooking then cover with a lid and leave to cook for 20 minutes on a low heat. Shake the pan gently now and again. The vegetables should cook in half an hour or so, but give them longer if they need it as they should be tender and quite cooked through.

Once done, the vegetables can sit happily for a while. Before serving, warm the vegetables, they need not be piping hot, and gently mix in the chopped dill, lemon juice and any seasoning required.

SEPTEMBER | OCTOBER | NOVEMBER

Apple popovers with cinnamon cream

"I heard about the Popover Café in New York a little while ago but haven't managed to get there as yet. These giant sized Yorkshire pudding style dishes they serve with savoury or sweet fillings sound delicious but are too big for my liking. So I've come up with a mini English version. I hope you like them". Maxine Golbourne

HANDS-ON TIME: 20 MINUTES PLUS 30 MINUTES CHILLING
COOKING TIME: 30 MINUTES
SERVES 6

FOR THE BATTER
1tsp vegetable oil
3 medium eggs
120ml milk
30g butter, melted
1tsp vanilla extract
70g plain flour
1/4 tsp salt
2tbsp caster sugar

FOR THE APPLES
30g butter
2 Cox's apples, peeled, cored and cut into slices around 1cm thick
2-3tbsp granulated sugar
1/4 tsp ground cinnamon

FOR THE CINNAMON CREAM
1tsp ground cinnamon
1tbsp brown sugar
200ml double cream

Preheat the oven to 200°C (400°F) gas mark 6 and lightly oil a 6-hole muffin tin. Put on the middle shelf of the oven to heat. To make the batter, mix together the ingredients until smooth then chill in the fridge for around 30 minutes.

Meanwhile, melt the butter in a heavy-based frying pan. Add the sliced apples, sugar and cinnamon and sauté over a gentle heat until tender. Once cooked, remove the muffin tin from the oven and divide the apples among the holes, pour over the batter and return to the oven.

Bake for around 20 minutes until the popovers are puffed and golden brown. Try not to open the oven door during the baking time otherwise they might collapse.

To make the cinnamon cream, warm the cinnamon and sugar in a small pan to bring out their flavours. Whip the double cream until it just holds its shape. Sprinkle over the warmed cinnamon sugar. Using two large spoons, scoop the cream into oval-shaped quenelles. The cinnamon sugar mixture should ripple naturally through the cream as you shape it.

Turn out the popovers onto serving plates and dust with icing sugar. Serve immediately with a spoonful of cinnamon cream.

Maxine Golbourne teaches at the Cookery School at Bordeaux Quay. She runs the Community Food Education Programme - the cornerstone of the Cookery School, among other workshops.

For Every Season

SEPTEMBER | OCTOBER | NOVEMBER

Fruit and nut crumble

"I've cooked this for lots of children and they all seem to enjoy it – it's a good way to get them to eat nuts and seeds as well as fruit. You can use any fruit in season – apple and blueberry is a favourite in our house". Louise Marchionne

HANDS-ON TIME: 15 MINUTES
COOKING TIME: 45–50 MINUTES
SERVES 4

FOR THE FILLING

3 apples
2 large pears
2tbsp good-quality blueberry jam
1-2tbsp golden caster sugar to taste

FOR THE CRUMBLE

50g jumbo oats
100g sunflower seeds
50g almonds
50g brazil nuts
50g pumpkin seeds
1tbsp sesame seeds
1tbsp golden caster sugar
25g butter or 2tsp sunflower oil

Preheat the oven to 190°C (375°F) gas 5. Peel and roughly chop the apples and pears. Mix together with the jam and transfer to a pie dish. Sprinkle over the sugar and bake in the oven for around 30 minutes until soft.

Meanwhile make the crumble topping. Put all the dry ingredients in a food processor and whiz together until roughly ground. Add the butter or oil. Whiz again until it starts to resemble a crumble topping. Sprinkle the crumble over the cooked fruit and return to the oven for around 15-20 minutes until golden brown. You can serve the crumble hot or cold. It makes an excellent breakfast with a spoonful of natural yoghurt.

cook's tip

When berries are in season, use a mixture of fresh blackberries, blackcurrants and blueberries instead of jam. This recipe is a hit with those who suffer from food allergies. Use fructose sugar instead of caster sugar, goat's butter and yoghurt instead of the cow's milk equivalent. Fructose sugar is three times sweeter than cane sugar so you can usually cut back on the amount of sugar in any recipe by at least half.

Louise Marchionne is a member of the Register of Allergy Therapists and a qualified Reflexologist. She practices out of the Enso Healing Rooms, 190 Cheltenham Road, Bristol, BS6 5RB www.fooditforyou.co.uk

For Every Season

SEPTEMBER | OCTOBER | NOVEMBER

Gingerbread

"It's 4 o' clock. The rain is lashing down, it's already dark and I'm cold. There's only one thing for it, I'm going to make a cake. This ginger cake has a fiery warmth to it – it's delicious eaten as soon as it's made but even better when wrapped tightly in foil and left for a few days. In this instance I can't wait for it to cool quick enough so I can have a huge slice and feel immediately happier and cosier". Carol Haines

HANDS-ON TIME: 20 MINUTES
COOKING TIME: AROUND 1 HOUR

FOR THE CAKE
250g butter plus extra for greasing
250g dark muscovado sugar
250g black treacle
300ml milk
2 eggs
100g stem ginger in syrup, finely chopped
375g plain flour
2tsp bicarbonate of soda
1tsp allspice
2tsp ground ginger

FOR THE ICING
5tbsp icing sugar
3tbsp ginger syrup from the jar

Preheat the oven to 160°C (325°F) gas mark 3. Grease and line a 23cm square baking tin (or use a roasting tin). Melt the butter, sugar and treacle in a pan over a gentle heat. Stir in the milk. The mix should be just warm to the touch. If not, leave to cool a little longer, then beat in the eggs. If the mixture is too warm, the eggs will scramble. Mix together the chopped ginger and all the dry ingredients in a large bowl and make a well in the centre. Pour the warm milk and egg mix into the well, then gradually draw the dry ingredients into the wet with a wooden spoon, until you have a thick, smooth batter.

Turn the batter into the prepared tin, then bake for 1 hour until risen and firm to the touch. The cake is cooked when a skewer inserted comes out clean.

Leave to cool in the tin. Once completely cool, turn out of the tin ready for icing, or wrap tightly in foil and keep for up to a week.

To make the icing, sift the icing sugar into a bowl and add the ginger syrup. Mix well until you have a smooth, runny icing. Once the cake has cooled, drizzle over the icing and cut into squares. If you're planning to let the cake mature for a while before eating, make the icing the day you plan to eat it.

Trained chef, Carol Haines teaches classes for both adults and children at the Cookery School at Bordeaux Quay. She runs her own catering company too.

SEPTEMBER | OCTOBER | NOVEMBER

And another thing...

Caramel apples and pears

Melt 50g each butter and sugar in a medium frying pan. Add 2 cored, sliced apples and 2 cored, sliced pears to the pan. Cook gently, turning occasionally until the fruit is soft and golden (about 10 minutes) Serve with....

...Mascarpone ice cream

Put 250g mascarpone, 250ml milk and 150g caster sugar in a bowl and whisk until thick and smooth. Transfer to an ice cream machine and churn until frozen. Scoop into a container and freeze until ready to serve. If you don't have a machine, put the container in the freezer and leave for 1-2 hours until nearly solid. Remove from the freezer, beat well with a wire whisk or electric beater until smooth then return to the freezer. Repeat the process twice more to break down ice crystals.

Winter

The thing about winter is that it does drag on a bit. In culinary terms this means that by January we are sick of root vegetables and are longing for the more delicate flavours and textures of spring. So we have to be constantly creative with the same vegetables, warm salads, soups, spicy tagines, vegetables roast and served with garlicky mayonnaise, or just the addition of a strong herb like rosemary or sage, all bring life and variety to the unassuming but reliable winter vegetable.

DECEMBER | JANUARY | FEBRUARY

Hot beetroot and apple salad with a warm horseradish dressing

"The earthy-sweet acidity of the beetroot is a great match for white fish or white meat. This is a lovely hot salad to give a pickle-sharpness to your cold meat and jacket potato".

Tamasin Day-Lewis

HANDS-ON TIME: 20 MINUTES
COOKING TIME: 40–50 MINUTES
SERVES 4

4 medium beetroot, skins on but cleaned
2 small sharp eating apples like Cox
4tbsp olive oil
1tbsp red wine vinegar
2tsp grated fresh horseradish or grated hot horseradish, to taste
Fresh dill or parsley

Preheat the oven to 190°C (375°F) gas mark 5. Bake the beetroots whole and wrapped tightly in foil in the oven. This will take about 40-50 minutes.

Five minutes before they are ready, grate the apple. Warm the olive oil and vinegar in a small pan and stir in the horseradish to taste. Season with salt and black pepper. Pour the dressing over the apple to stop it discolouring. Remove the beetroot from the foil and peel with a knife, holding the hot beetroot on the prongs of a fork to make it easier. Grate the beetroot on the large grater holes onto the pile of apple and toss it all together. Scatter over your herbs and serve.

DECEMBER | JANUARY | FEBRUARY

Roasted guinea fowl with braised chicory and white wine sauce

By Michael Caines

HANDS-ON TIME: 30 MINUTES
COOKING TIME: 1 HOUR 10 MINUTES
SERVES 4

FOR THE BIRD

2kg guinea fowl
1 garlic bulb, peeled and halved around its middle
Few thyme sprigs
Few rosemary sprigs
Extra virgin olive oil

FOR THE CHICORY

Butter
1 onion, peeled and sliced
250ml chicken stock
1tbsp sugar
Bouquet garni (celery stalk, parsley stalk, thyme and bay leaf bound with leek and string)
4 heads chicory, outer leaves removed

FOR THE SAUCE

25g plus 90g unsalted butter (to finish)
1 small shallot, peeled and sliced
1 garlic clove, peeled and chopped
Thyme sprigs
Bay leaf
50ml dry white wine
250ml chicken stock or guinea fowl stock
2tbsp cream
Fresh tarragon

Preheat the oven to 190°C (375°F) gas mark 5. Season the inside of the guinea fowl with salt and black pepper and stuff with 1/2 bulb garlic and the thyme and rosemary sprigs. Put in a roasting tray, drizzle over some oil and season again. Roast for around 45 minutes, basting occasionally.

Once cooked, remove from the tin and set aside to rest for 15 minutes. Skim the fat from the roasting tin and transfer the remaining juices to a jug.

While the guinea fowl is cooking, prepare the braised chicory. Melt 25g butter in a shallow ovenproof pan or a roasting tin and add the sliced onion and 1tsp salt. Cook gently until soft, but not browned. Add 500ml water, the stock, sugar and bouquet garni. Add the chicory and bring to the boil then cover with foil and transfer to the oven for around 30 minutes, until tender. Remove from the oven and cool. Once cool, cut the chicory in half lengthways. Melt a knob of butter in a frying pan, add the chicory halves and cook over gentle heat, turning until both sides are golden and caramelized.

To make the sauce, melt 25g butter in a pan and add the sliced shallots and chopped garlic. Cook over a gentle heat until softened. Add a few thyme sprigs and the bay leaf and cook for a further 2 minutes.

Add the wine, bring to the boil and bubble gently until almost no liquid remains. Don't let it burn. Add the stock and bubble again until the liquid is reduced by half, then add the cream and whisk in the remaining butter. Add the meat juices and season to taste. Just before serving, pick and chop the tarragon leaves and add to the sauce at the last minute.

serving suggestion

To serve, put two pieces of caramelised chicory in the middle of each plate, with two pieces guinea fowl (half a breast and either a thigh or a drumstick). Pour over the hot sauce and serve with roasted vegetables on the side.

Founder of Michael Caines restaurants and co-founder of Abode Hotels, Michael Caines is Executive Chef at Gidleigh Park Country House Hotel, Chagford, Devon, TQ13 8HH www.gidleigh.com; www.michaelcaines.com

DECEMBER | JANUARY | FEBRUARY

Muscovado heaven

"It MUST be dark muscovado sugar that you use in this recipe. Other brown sugars do not have the rich treacly taste". Prue Leith

**HANDS-ON TIME: 5 MINUTES
PLUS 30 MINUTES CHILLING
SERVES 4**

**300ml low-fat natural yoghurt
300ml thick-ish cold custard made with custard powder, but no sugar
3tbsp dark muscovado sugar**

serving suggestion
You can put a dollop of stewed fruit compote at the bottom of the cups.

Mix together the yoghurt and cold custard. Divide among four serving glasses or cups. Sprinkle each heavily with muscovado sugar.

Leave in the fridge for 30 minutes until the sugar starts to dissolve.

If you like crunch, add another small sprinkling of sugar on top before serving.

DECEMBER | JANUARY | FEBRUARY

Squash and coconut gratinée with a hazelnut crust

"This hearty winter bake uses the deep orange flesh of crown prince squash, stores of which should last well into winter after the autumn harvest. We suggest a simple watercress salad to accompany and balance the richness. Squeeze a good orange over the watercress for an easy salad dressing". Mark Evans

**HANDS-ON TIME: 30 MINUTES;
COOKING TIME: 1 HR 20 MINUTES;
SERVES 6**

2 -3kg crown prince squash
250g potatoes, peeled
400g can coconut milk
1tsp ground fenugreek
1tsp ground fennel
1/2 tsp salt
4 garlic cloves, peeled and finely chopped
2.5cm piece fresh root ginger, peeled and finely chopped
1 lemongrass stalk, outer layer removed and finely chopped
2 rosemary sprigs, leaves removed and finely chopped

FOR THE TOPPING

4 shallots, peeled and finely chopped
300g hazelnuts, roasted, skinned and roughly chopped
4 rosemary sprigs, leaves removed and finely chopped
150g pecorino or parmesan, grated (optional)
2tbsp olive oil

Preheat the oven to 150°C (300°F) gas mark 2.

Using a large knife, cut the squash in half and then cut each half into four slices. Each slice should be around 4cm thick. Scoop out the seeds and pith. Use a small paring knife to remove the tough olive green skin.

Finely slice the squash using the slicing attachment on a food processor if you have one. Otherwise, slice each piece by hand making sure each is no more than 1mm thick. Slice the potatoes to the same thickness and put both in a large mixing bowl.

In a separate bowl, mix together the coconut milk, fenugreek, fennel and salt. Add the chopped garlic, ginger, lemongrass and rosemary.

Pour the coconut mixture over the squash and potatoes. Season thoroughly with salt and black pepper and transfer to a baking dish measuring approximately 30cm x 20cm x 5cm.

Pat down firmly to make sure the vegetables are coated with the coconut milk.

Bake in the preheated oven for 1 hour 20 minutes until tender when pierced with a knife.

To make the topping, mix together the chopped shallots, hazelnuts, rosemary and pecorino, if using. Season with black pepper and mix in the olive oil to bind.

After 1 hour cooking, remove the gratinée from the oven and spread over the topping with a palette knife. Return to the oven and bake for a further 20 minutes.

DECEMBER | JANUARY | FEBRUARY

Apple and calvados pudding with sticky toffee calvados sauce

"This pudding is fiery with calvados, added to warm one up on cold wintry nights".

Rachel Demuth

HANDS-ON TIME: AROUND 30 MINUTES
COOKING TIME: 45–50 MINUTES
SERVES 6

FOR THE APPLE

2tbsp caster sugar
450g apples, peeled, cored and thinly sliced
15g unsalted butter
4tbsp calvados

FOR THE SPONGE

100g unsalted butter plus extra for greasing
100g caster sugar
4tbsp calvados
3 eggs
100g self-raising flour
1tsp baking powder
1/2 tsp ground cinnamon
85g ground almonds
85g fresh white breadcrumbs

FOR THE SAUCE

55g soft brown sugar
30g golden syrup
30g unsalted butter
55ml double cream
2-4tbsp calvados

Preheat the oven to 200°C (400°F) gas mark 6. Grease and line a 20.5cm square cake tin with baking parchment.

To make the apple layer, put the sugar in a medium pan with 1tbsp water and heat until the sugar is dissolved and bubbling. Add the sliced apples and butter, stir briefly then add the calvados. Simmer gently for around 5 minutes until the liquid has evaporated. The apples should be translucent but still retain their shape. Spread the mix evenly over the base of the cake tin.

To make the sponge, cream together the butter and sugar until smooth. Add the calvados and whisk in the eggs. Sift in the flour together with the baking powder and ground cinnamon. Fold in the ground almonds and breadcrumbs.

Spread the sponge mix over the apples, smooth the top with a spatula and bake in the preheated oven for 25-30 minutes until golden and risen. Remove from the oven and leave to cool slightly.

To make the sauce, put the sugar, golden syrup and butter in a pan and heat gently until the sugar has dissolved. Stir in the cream and calvados.

Serve the pudding, with plenty of sauce and a generous helping of cream, ice cream or even custard.

cook's tip

To make an especially indulgent sticky pudding, make a double quantity of the sauce recipe. Once the pudding is cooked, pierce all over with a skewer and pour over half the sauce. Set aside for a day to give the pudding time to absorb the sauce then serve as above.

DECEMBER | JANUARY | FEBRUARY

Sweet and sour mussels with chilli

"It's hard to beat a good dish of mussels steamed in wine and parsley but this might get close. The fragrance of Asian herbs make me to want to go and cook shellfish and although there is a lot of flavour in this dish, it doesn't overpower the mussels and their texture works really well here. This is a great, warm, spicy dish to share". Mitchell Tonks

HANDS-ON TIME: 20 MINUTES
COOKING TIME: AROUND 20 MINUTES
SERVES 2

1kg live mussels
2tbsp groundnut oil
1 onion, peeled and finely sliced
2 garlic cloves, peeled and finely sliced
1tbsp fresh root ginger, peeled and finely chopped
2-4 red chillies, to taste, de-seeded and finely sliced
150ml white wine vinegar
5tbsp sugar
Splash of fish sauce
Juice of a lime
Handful coriander leaves, finely chopped
Small handful basil leaves, roughly torn

De-beard the mussels and scrub to get rid of any barnacles and grit.

Put the mussels in a large pan with a little water and cook over a medium heat until the shells open. Discard any that remain closed then set aside. Heat the oil in a large frying pan and add the onion, garlic, ginger and chillies. Cook over a gentle heat until softened.

Add the vinegar and sugar and stir well to dissolve. Season to taste with a little more vinegar or sugar if needed.

Add a few drops of fish sauce, increase the heat and simmer for 2-3 minutes. Tip the mussels and their juices into the frying pan and stir well to create a sticky coating over the mussels.

Squeeze over the lime juice and add the herbs. Serve hot or chilled.

Mitchell Tonks is a restaurateur, food writer and chef. He owns The Seahorse restaurant in Dartmouth www.seahorserestaurant.co.uk

For Every Season | 75

DECEMBER | JANUARY | FEBRUARY

Vindaloo ice cream with mango and poppadom tuiles

"The Victorians used to eat both savoury and sweet ice-creams. The appeal of this pudding lies in the contrast between the heat of the spices and the cool ice cream".

Chris Wicks

HANDS-ON TIME: 40 MINUTES
COOKING TIME: AROUND 15 MINUTES
SERVES 8–10

630ml whole milk
55g milk powder
120g golden caster sugar
6 medium egg yolks
2tbsp vindaloo curry paste

FOR THE POPPADOM TUILE

55g rice flour
55g chickpea flour
100g caster sugar
100g butter
100g egg white

FOR THE MANGO

1 ripe mango, peeled and finely diced
Juice of a lime
1tbsp chopped mint

TO MAKE THE ICE CREAM

Boil together the milk, milk powder and half the sugar. Whisk the remaining sugar together with the egg yolks.

Pour the hot milk onto the egg mixture whisking vigorously. Rinse the pan then return the mixture and cook gently, stiring constantly until the mixture is thickened and coats the back of a wooden spoon. Strain, cover with clingfilm and leave to cool. Stir in the curry paste then tip into an ice cream maker and churn. Freeze below -18°C

TO MAKE THE POPPADOM TUILES

Preheat the oven to 180°C (350°F) gas mark 4.

Mix all the ingredients to a fine paste. Leave to rest for 20 minutes then spread in circles of approx 6cm in diameter onto a silicone mat. Bake in the preheated oven for 3-4 minutes, then remove from the oven and lift onto a rolling pin or a ramekin to bend into shape. Try and work as quickly as you can to be able to bend the poppadoms into shape before they dry out and harden.

Store in a sealed container for up to two days in a cool dry place.

TO MAKE THE MANGO

Mix together chopped mango with lime juice to taste and the chopped mint. Chill before serving.

Serve a scoop of ice cream with a tuile and a spoonful of mango on the side.

DECEMBER | JANUARY | FEBRUARY

Five root soup

"This is not a smooth blended soup, but a broth packed full of little pieces of root veg. Their flavours remain more distinct this way, which is very pleasing. Enriched with plenty of smoky bacon and finished with grated cheese, this is a fabulous, sustaining, salt-of-the-earth sort of dish. Make sure you cut the vegetables small, and keep the pieces all the same size". Gill Meller

HANDS-ON TIME: AROUND 20 MINUTES
COOKING TIME: 40–45 MINUTES
SERVES 4

1tbsp olive oil
200g smoked streaky bacon or pancetta, cut into small dice
1 large onion, peeled and finely chopped
150g carrots, peeled and diced
150g swede, peeled and diced
150g potatoes, peeled and diced
150g parsnip, peeled and diced
150g celeriac, peeled and diced
1.1l light vegetable, ham or chicken stock
About 100g grated mature cheddar, to garnish

Heat the olive oil in a large pan over a medium heat

Add the bacon and cook gently until the fat starts to run and the bacon starts to brown. Add the chopped onion and sweat gently for a further 10-15 minutes until soft and golden.

Add the diced vegetables, stir briefly to coat then cover the pan and let the whole mixture sweat and soften for around 10 minutes. Add the stock and increase the heat to a simmer. Cover and cook for a further 15 minutes until the vegetables are tender. Taste the soup and season accordingly. Ladle into warmed bowls, top each with a little pile of grated cheese and serve immediately, with some thick pieces of toast.

Gill Meller is head chef at River Cottage HQ, River Cottage, Park Farm, Trinity Hill, Axminster, Devon, EX13 5NX www.rivercottage.net

DECEMBER | JANUARY | FEBRUARY

Repapalos

"This marvellous pudding comes from the south west of Spain and is an unexpected and delicious way to use up stale bread. It is also rather good for breakfast". Sophie Grigson

Sophie Grigson has written over 14 books to go with her many TV series. She has written columns and articles for numerous newspapers and magazines and was awarded the Guild of Food Writers Cookery Journalist Award in 2001. She is a regular feature at the Demo Kitchen at Bristol's Organic Food Festival

HANDS-ON TIME: 10 MINUTES PLUS 30 MINUTES RESTING
COOKING TIME: AROUND 30 MINUTES
SERVES 8

100g stale breadcrumbs (made from bread that is 2-4 days old, crust included)
4-5 large eggs, lightly beaten
Olive oil, or a mixture of olive and sunflower oil, for deep frying
1.75l full-cream milk
Pared zest of 1 orange, cut in wide strips
2 cinnamon sticks
100g caster sugar
Ground cinnamon

Beat the breadcrumbs with enough of the beaten eggs to form a thick batter of dropping consistency. Leave to rest for 30 minutes.

Heat the oil to 170°C (325°F). At this temperature a piece of bread dropped into the oil should fizz gently. Test the batter by cooking one experimental dumpling. Drop a generous teaspoon of the mixture into the oil and fry for 2-4 minutes until golden. It should puff up slightly to form a nice, fairly neatly shaped ball or sphere. If it stays irredeemably lumpy and over-solid, add a little more egg to the batter to loosen it. If it disintegrates, thicken the batter with a few more breadcrumbs.

Once the batter is right, start frying seriously, as above, dropping teaspoons of it into the hot oil and turning the dumplings so that they cook evenly. Never over-crowd the pan. Drain thoroughly on kitchen paper.

Put the cooled repapalos into a clean pan and add all the remaining ingredients except the ground cinnamon. Bring to the boil and simmer for 15 minutes. Spoon the dumplings into a bowl, pour over the hot milk, dust with ground cinnamon and leave to cool. Serve chilled (I think they improve with a day or so's keeping).

DECEMBER | JANUARY | FEBRUARY

Beef featherblade with lentils and green sauce

"A dish cooked by mother many years ago has lingered in my memory and appears on the menu regularly in several variations. A piece of shoulder of beef cooked very slowly on the gentlest heat for a considerable length of time until it attains remarkable tenderness. The recipe we love and cook most is that given below". Jeremy Lee

**HANDS-ON TIME: 30 MINUTES
COOKING TIME: 4 1/2 - 6 1/2 HOURS
SERVES 10–12**

FOR THE BEEF
**6tbsp olive oil
A piece of featherblade weighing approx 2.5kg
150g unsalted butter
6 sage leaves
Generous sprig each of thyme and rosemary
10 garlic cloves, unpeeled**

FOR THE LENTILS
**250g Puy lentils
1 small carrot
1 small onion
1 stick of celery
2 cloves garlic
Bay leaf**

FOR THE GREEN SAUCE
**1 garlic clove
4 anchovy fillets
1tsp capers
A tight fistful of picked flat leaf parsley, leaves picked and washed
2tbsp olive oil
1tbsp very good red wine vinegar**

Heat 5tbsp oil in a heavy bottomed pot. Season the beef with salt and black pepper and rub in well. Add the meat to the pan and leave to sit until darkened. Turn occasionally until the beef is marvellously crusted all over.

Remove the beef and wipe the pan, leaving any crispy bits stuck to the base. Add the butter, remaining oil, herbs and garlic then return the beef to the pan and mix together. Add a cup of water, cover and reduce the heat to a murmur. Leave to cook quietly for 4-6 hours until tender, adding a little water now and then to keep the whole thing merry.

Towards the end of cooking time, turn your attention towards the lentils. Rinse well in a sieve under cold running water. Peel and finely chop the carrot, onion, celery and garlic. Heat the oil in a large pan and add the chopped vegetables. Fry gently, stirring, for 10 minutes. Stir in the lentils and bay leaf and add enough water to cover. Bring to a simmer and cook, covered, for around 45 minutes until tender.

Meanwhile, make the green sauce. Peel and finely chop the garlic. Chop the anchovies and capers and mix with the garlic. Finely chop the parsley leaves and mix into the garlic mixture. Transfer to a bowl and add the oil and vinegar. Stir together well.

Remove the beef to a splendid dish. Add a little water to the pan, increase the heat and stir well to dislodge any scraps stuck to the base. Add the warm lentils and the sauce. Pour the lentils and sauce over the beef and take triumphantly to table where folks can help themselves.

Jeremy Lee is head chef at the Blueprint Café, Design Museum, Shad Thames, London SE1 2YD www.blueprintcafe.co.uk

Venison faggots

"I appreciate that not everyone has access to venison offal. For those of you who do, read on and enjoy – or alternatively, use pork offal". Gill Meller

HANDS-ON TIME: 40 MINUTES PLUS 15 MINUTES SOAKING PLUS 1 HOUR CHILLING;
COOKING TIME: 40 MINUTES
SERVES 6

- 500g very fresh venison liver
- 1 venison heart
- 1 set of venison lights (lungs)
- 250g fat pork belly, roughly chopped
- 250g bacon pieces
- 1 onion, peeled and finely chopped
- 150g fresh breadcrumbs
- 60ml port or brandy
- 4 juniper berries, crushed
- 2 garlic cloves, peeled and crushed
- 1tbsp flat-leafed parsley, finely chopped
- 1tbsp thyme leaves, finely chopped
- Pared zest of half an orange, finely chopped
- A good pinch of nutmeg
- Pre-soaked pork or venison caul fat (ask your butcher)

Peel any membrane from the liver and trim out any tough ventricles. Do the same with the heart.

Trim, cube and soak the lights in fresh water for 15 minutes. Mix together the pork belly, bacon, onion, liver, heart and lung and put the whole lot through a mincer on the medium plate (5mm). Transfer to a bowl, add all the other ingredients except the caul fat and mix well.

Chill the mixture for 30 minutes then divide into balls each weighing approximately 150g. Wrap each ball in a sheet of caul fat (see cook's tip) and chill for a further 30 minutes.

Heat a heavy-based frying pan over a medium-high heat, add the faggots (don't overcrowd the pan) and reduce the heat to medium. Gently fry the faggots until golden brown on all sides and cooked through. Alternatively, bake in the oven at 180°C (350°F) Gas mark 4 for 40 minutes, with a little stock in the bottom of the roasting tip to keep them moist.

cook's tip

Don't worry if you can't get hold of caul fat. The faggots work well without. Make sure you pack them tightly with your hands before you chill them.

If you don't have a mincer, ask your butcher to prepare and mince the offal.

Gill Meller is head chef at River Cottage HQ, River Cottage, Park Farm, Trinity Hill, Axminster, Devon, EX13 5NX www.rivercottage.net

DECEMBER | JANUARY | FEBRUARY

Roast root vegetable gratin

"This is one for the farmer's market, the vegetable box or a good fruit and vegetable store who make local, organic and seasonal a priority in sourcing their produce. A combination of three or four vegtables is good: think butternut squash, sweet potato, carrot, celeriac, turnip, swede, parsnip, but not potato". *Barny Haughton*

HANDS-ON TIME: 30 MINUTES
COOKING TIME: 1 HOUR 35 MINUTES
SERVES 6

FOR THE ROASTED VEGETABLES
Around 4kg unpeeled vegetables
2 onions, peeled and sliced
25ml rapeseed or sunflower oil
200g soft breadcrumbs made from stale bread
100g grated parmesan (cheddar is fine)
1tbsp thyme leaves, chopped
2 garlic cloves, peeled and finely chopped
1tsp fennel seeds, crushed

FOR THE AIOLI
3-5 plump garlic cloves, depending on size and taste, peeled
2 egg yolks
1/2tsp salt
3tsp white wine vinegar
300ml extra virgin olive oil
Juice of half a lemon

Preheat oven to 180°C (350°F) gas mark 4. Peel and chop the vegetables into uneven but similarly sized chunks about 2cm square. Mix together in a bowl with the onions and oil and season generously with salt and black pepper. Spread loosely on a roasting tray and put in the oven. Roast for about 1 hour 20 minutes, turning every 20 minutes or so, scraping the pan as you do, until evenly light brown and cooked.

Meanwhile, mix together the breadcrumbs, parmesan, chopped thyme, garlic and fennel seeds. A food processor is good for this, but don't whiz the mix too finely. Set aside.

To make the aioli, put the peeled garlic on a large chopping board, sprinkle over a pinch of salt and crush vigorously with the flat side of a large knife then chop finely.

Put the egg yolks, salt and vinegar in a bowl and, using a wire whisk, establish a fine, gentle drizzle of olive oil into the egg mixture, whisking constantly. Adding the oil too quickly will cause it to split. Once it is thick and creamy you can add the oil more quickly.

Add the minced garlic, beat well, adjust the seasoning and add a squeeze of lemon juice.

Just before serving, sprinkle the breadcrumb mixture over the top of the vegetables and return to the oven for 15 minutes. Serve with aioli and plainly boiled cabbage. Lovely.

Barny Haughton is chef-proprietor of Bordeaux Quay, V-Shed, Canons Way, Bristol BS1 5UH www.bordeaux-quay.co.uk

DECEMBER | JANUARY | FEBRUARY

Seven vegetable couscous

"This dish is great on its own or with a couple of fillets of red mullet for a more substantial serving". Freddy Bird

HANDS-ON TIME: AROUND 30 MINUTES
COOKING TIME: AROUND 45 MINUTES
SERVES 6-8

Olive oil
4 red onions, peeled and sliced
6 garlic cloves, peeled and chopped
Thumb-sized piece root ginger, peeled and finely chopped
2tsp cumin seeds, toasted and ground
3tsp coriander seeds, toasted and ground
Good pinch saffron
Pinch dried chilli
Pinch unsmoked paprika
2 red peppers, de-seeded and cut into quarters
2 celery sticks, cut into 4
2 large carrots, peeled and cut into 4
1 small white cabbage, chopped into 8 small wedges
1/2 butternut squash, peeled and cut into chunks
4 small turnips, halved
1/2 celeriac, cut into wedges
Vegetable stock
Fresh coriander

Heat 3tbsp olive oil in a large pan and add the red onions. Cook, stirring, until softened and lightly golden. Add the garlic, ginger and all the spices and fry for a further 5 minutes. Season with salt and black pepper.

Add the chopped vegetables to the caramelised onions and cook for a few minutes, stirring gently. Add just enough stock to cover. Bring to the boil then turn the heat right down and simmer until the vegetables are just tender.

Just before serving, scatter over plenty of chopped coriander. Serve with steamed couscous, ensuring everyone gets each of the seven vegetables and plenty of broth.

cook's tip
Make sure the vegetables are chopped into same sized pieces to ensure they cook at the same rate.

Freddy Bird is senior sous-chef at Bordeaux Quay, V-Shed, Canons Way, Bristol BS1 5UH www.bordeaux-quay.co.uk

DECEMBER | JANUARY | FEBRUARY

And another thing...

Chicory

A vegetable normally eaten as a salad – perhaps with walnuts, chopped hard boiled egg and chives, is quite different when cooked; braised in a little water and butter, its bitter flavour becomes softened and sweet. It's the perfect vegetable to go with almost any fish, but is particularly good with sea bass.

Red cabbage

At its best finely chopped, seasoned with salt, pepper and a few cloves and cooked in a low oven with a chopped cooking apple and onion. A splash of red wine vinegar and a pinch of sugar at the end helps preserve its colour and balance the flavour. Serve as the main act or with simply roasted meat.

Quinces

Knobbly and apple-like, don't be fooled into eating them raw. Prepare in the same way as apples or pears and add to crumbles, pies or poach them in sugar syrup. Heat together equal quantities of sugar and water (or use a mixture of water and wine – pudding wine works especially well here) until the sugar has dissolved. Drop in the peeled, cored and quartered quinces and poach gently for around 1 hour until tender. Boil the syrup to reduce if you need to, then pour over the quinces and serve.

Booklist

"You don't need shelves of cookery books. A few well-researched volumes will stand you in good stead for any occasion. It's a personal choice of course, but here are some of my best-loved favourites". Barny Haughton

Roast Chicken and Other Stories
by Simon Hopkinson with Lindsay Bareham
This book takes 15 or so ingredients and gives you ten (or so) dishes to make with each one. That makes it sound rather dull. It isn't: It's one of the most appealing cookery books I've read.

River Café Cookbook Easy
by Rose Gray and Ruth Rogers
And they really are easy recipes: simple, delicious and very few use more than four ingredients. But they do have to be absolutely the best ingredients.

Rick Stein's Fruits of the Sea
by Rick Stein
Of all the hundreds of seafood cookery books written over the past decade, this book has never been bettered: incredibly informative, modestly presented but inspiring recipes covering every fish you are likely to ever eat - and every recipe works (I have done them all).

French Provincial Cooking
by Elizabeth David
If you haven't got this book, buy it. It's not just that Elizabeth David is probably the most important cookery writer in the English speaking language or that the recipes reflect the kind of food culture we all love - and now need more than ever – but also that it is written with an authority, elegance, erudition and wit which makes most other cookery books seem almost pointless.

Simple French Food
by Richard Olney
A book to read for pleasure. Olney reflects on how the simplest dishes come from a complex tapestry of tradition, provenance, ritual and passion. If you cook a few of Olney's recipes – which themselves read like little watercolours: few brush strokes, perfectly articulated – then so much the better.

The Classic Italian Cookbook
by Marcella Hazan
No pictures, but the recipes don't need any, and no Italian cookbook better demonstrates the significance of regional cooking: as a way of life, as a philosophy, as a jealously guarded tradition.

Real Food
by Nigel Slater
I could have chosen just about any of Nigel Slater's books because they are all maddeningly brilliant. This one was first published in 1998, but it might as well have been written yesterday.

Green Seasons Cookbook
by Rachel Demuth
There isn't a dish in this vegetarian cookbook which the most entrenched carnivore wouldn't love. And since we should all eat less meat (about 80% less), this book offers a delightful and informative (especially about how properly to use herbs, spices, nuts, seeds and soya) introduction to this under-valued dimension of gastronomy.

Wild Garlic, Gooseberries and Me
by Denis Cotter
I chose this book because it's full of stories, it's vegetarian, the recipes are faultless and delicious, the pictures and especially the hardback cover

are lovely, and because Cotter writes about broad beans as if he was writing about God.

Sophie Grigson's Meat Course
by Sophie Grigson

In a culinary world dominated by chefs, there is an odd paradox: although restaurant and home cooking have become oddly blurred, the two activities are in fact utterly different. This book is for home cooks and chefs who ought to know what home cooking is about and maybe don't. The recipes are wonderful and artlessly precise and cover just about every cut of meat you are likely to use.

Beyond Baked Beans
by Fiona Beckett

If you already know how to cook reasonably well (i.e. you can make good soup, good bread and cook Christmas dinner for 20 people without getting cross) then you don't need this book. Its target readership is students but for anyone who hasn't got their head round the basics of cooking, this is the best possible introduction.

Organisations and initiatives

"Here are a few organisations that offer practical information and advice on a variety of subjects from sourcing sustainable local food to insulating your home".

Amy Robinson

www.fishonline.org
Fish Online is the Marine Conservation Society guide to which fish we should be eating and which are unsustainable and should be avoided.

www.rainforest-alliance.org
The Rainforest Alliance works to conserve biodiversity and preserve sustainable livelihoods. They certify a variety of products from coffee to paper.

www.recyclenow.com
The Recycle Now website is full of information and advice on recycling and home composting.

www.soilassociation.org
The Soil Association is an environmental charity promoting sustainable organic farming and championing human health. They also certify organic products.

www.wrap.org.uk
WRAP helps individuals, businesses and local authorities to reduce waste and recycle more, making better use of resources and helping to tackle climate change.

www.eca.gov.uk
Enhanced Capital Allowance is a Government programme that provides businesses with enhanced tax relief for investments in equipment that meets published energy-saving criteria.

www.fairtrade.org.uk
The Fairtrade Foundation works with businesses, community groups and individuals in the developing world to deliver sustainable livelihoods for farmers and their communities. They certify products imported from these countries.

www.fsc.org
The Forest Stewardship Council is an independent, non-governmental, not-for-profit organisation which promotes responsible management of the world's forests. They certify a range of products of wood origin from notepads to garden furniture.

www.energysavingtrust.org.uk
The Energy Saving Trust provides free impartial tailored advice to help save money and fight climate change by reducing CO2 emissions from homes.

Amy Robinson is Sustainable Development Manager of Bordeaux Quay, V-Shed, Canons Way, Bristol BS1 5UH www.bordeaux-quay.co.uk

Recipe Index

A
Aligot, 62
Apple and calvados pudding with sticky toffee calvados sauce, 74
Apple and sweet geranium jelly, 60
Apple popovers with cinnamon cream, 65
Asparagus and potato frittata, 28
Asparagus with hollandaise sauce, 32
Assiette de crudités Maman Blanc, 44
autumn raspberry jam, Six minute, 58

B
Baked sea bream, as in the Balearics, 36
bean stew, Italian, 18
Beef
Beef featherblade with lentils and green sauce, 79

beetroot and apple salad with a warm horseradish dressing, Hot, 70
Broad beans, 50

C
Cabbage, red, 83
Cabbage with bacon, 57
Cakes
A proper chocolate cake, 24
Carrot cake, 26
Gingerbread, 67
Simple rosewater cake, 37

Caramel apples and pears, 68
Carrot cake, 26
cherry jelly, Sparkling summer, 48
Chicory, 83
Chicken
Lemon and thyme roast chicken, 63
Moroccan chicken tagine, 21

Chocolate cake, A proper, 24
Courgette and goat's cheese tart with beetroot, watercress and broad bean salad, 34

D, E, F
Fish
Baked sea bream, as in the Balearics, 36
John Dory with kale, cockle and blood orange vinaigrette, 25
Pollack Grenobloise, 31

Roasted garlic and parsley fish stew, 49
Steamed mussels with tomato and tarragon, 42
Sweet and sour mussels with chilli, 75
Sweet and sour shrimp and pineapple soup, 41
Sweetcorn and brown shrimp fritters, 53

Five root soup, 77
Fruit and nut crumble, 66
fruit salad with sweet geranium leaves, Summer, 39

G
Game
Pasta with wild mushrooms and hare, 55
Pheasant casserole with ceps, pancetta and chestnuts, 61
Roasted guinea fowl with braised chicory and white wine sauce, 71
Venison faggots, 80

Garden salad of almost raw vegetables with goat's cheese, 47
Gazpacho, 35
Gingerbread, 67
Globe artichokes, 50
guinea fowl with braised chicory and white wine sauce, Roasted, 71

H, I
ice cream with mango and poppadom tuiles, Vindaloo, 76
Italian bean stew, 18

J
Jam and other preserves
Apple and sweet geranium jelly, 60
Six minute autumn raspberry jam, 58
Fresh rhubarb and orange relish, 46

John Dory with kale, cockle and blood orange vinaigrette, 25

K
Kidneys and bacon on toast with a little devilled sauce, 54

L
Lamb
Lamb, olive and aubergine stew, 38
Spring lamb with anchovy mayonnaise and hors d'oeuvres, 27

Leeks vinaigrette, 32
Lemon and thyme roast chicken, 63